Oral & Bernadette,
Continue to
a blessing to the
of the
Lord!)

For *these reasons* shall a man leave his father and mother and cleave to his wife…

A divine revelation on marriage, sexuality, dating and relationships

Rev. Nathan R. Byrd

5/24/08

xulon PRESS

"Celebrating Celibacy" Setting the standard for sexuality, marriage and relationships in the new millennium

a.k.a. For these reasons shall a man leave his father and mother and cleave to his wife...
A divine revelation on marriage, sexuality, dating and relationships

Copyright © 2003 by Rev. Nathan R. Byrd

For These Reasons Shall A Man Leave His Father and Mother and Cleave To His Wife...
by Rev. Nathan R. Byrd

Printed in the United States of America

ISBN 1-594671-69-9

Unless otherwise indicated, Bible quotations are taken from New King James Version of the Bible. Copyright © 1982 by Thomas Nelson, Inc.

Library of Congress Cataloging-in-Publication Data
Byrd, Nathan R. 1961-
    p. cm.

TXu 1-023-335 2001

Xulon Press
www.XulonPress.com

Xulon Press books are available in bookstores everywhere,
and on the Web at www.XulonPress.com.

Acknowledgements

To God my Father, thank you for sitting me down on the couch that beautiful spring afternoon and giving me the revelation I needed to continue on...to this point.

To my wife whom I did not know during the writing of this book, my dear Maria you are the answer to a very, very specific prayer.

To my son Court, if I could package your energy and sell it... needless to say, I'd be rich.

To my next door neighbor Scott, thanks for your red pen.

To my church family, thanks for your early vote of confidence.

To my brother Danny, thanks for always being so positive concerning my endeavors.

To my sister Sheila...things are about to get busy!

To my Dad...thanks and see you soon!

Dedicated to
the greatest woman I've ever known
Edwena Byrd
1930-1995

For these reasons...

"Sex is not a prerequisite..."

M. L. Asuncion

Preface

When the question is asked, "How important is a relationship to you right now?" the answers vary but seem to relate the same underlying thought. From the women you hear, "I've given up," "It doesn't really matter right now," "If it happens it happens," or "I hang out with my friends so I don't think about it." Most of the answers suggest that there is very little hope left in the area of a meaningful lasting relationship. From the men you hear "I like dating," "I don't want to be tied down," "I'm not ready to commit," "I haven't found the right lady," or "I'm having too much fun," and most of their answers suggest that a relationship is a task or an unwanted responsibility.

With these opinions being so dominant in our society how can we ever get to the point of marriage, commitment, and family? Men and women are so far from each other mentally and emotionally that combining the two is like mixing oil and water, they can be in the same jar but they remain separate.

Webster's Collegiate Dictionary describes a relationship as a natural or logical association between two or more people or things; connection; a connection of persons by blood or marriage. Though I agree with the definition, it seems that the methods and rules relative to relationships have changed drastically in this day and age from 40 years ago. We seem to have attached to the meaning some very pessimistic undertones that suggest burden, hardship, and impossibility. Since this culture's psychology and definition about relationships has changed we are more likely to view them as something we prefer to avoid. However, we'll take it if we get the sense that we will have the fairy tale scenario and we have the guarantee of living happily every after.

With that in mind, the books and studies and counselors of the world cannot take away the fear that grips most that walk down the isle, for their final 'single' stroll, to say "I do". Then again nowadays most say, "I do until" or "I do, but sign this agreement just in case I don't later" or their vows amount to "I'll try my best, but there's no guarantees." Marriage, being the actual fiber of the family, the essential foundation for child rearing, and the stability of the community as well as the church needs to be re-established. So that it will become desired rather than despised, enjoyed rather than endured, and relished rather than relinquished. Or else in a generation or two, we will be without the God instituted standard from which families are birthed.

What will happen to society without marriage? Take a moment to think about it. Think of the indulgence, the binges, the frustration, the violence, the rape, the perversity, the disease, the instability, the broken lives, the fragmented hearts, the confused children, the homosexuality, the dissolving of gender, the condition of the community, the frailty of the church. Some cultures have done well to preserve *marriage* but have similar problems when it comes to *relationships*. But in capitalistic societies and in capitalistic minds, marriage is only a hindrance to living and enjoying "my life".

But more importantly, we have an issue with God that needs to be dealt with. After we have made all of our excuses for why we can't live with anyone permanently or commit to another imperfect person or why we feel like with the statistics (about marriages) we would rather not even try it or we tried it before and we will never try it again; there is still the God issue. God has an issue with us breaking his rules and ignoring his ideals concerning sex and the relationship between men and women. What do we do with **God** and his issue? What do we do with the Bible that he left that has stood the test of time? What do we do with the internal, innate feelings that tell us something is wrong with this picture? What do we do with the STD, HIV, homosexuality issues and beyond? Better yet what do we tell our children? What do we say to the child that asks, "How did *I* come to be if it takes a mommy and a daddy to make a child and all I have is two moms or two dads?

The main reason behind why we are struggling in society with the issues surrounding sex, marriage, dating and relationships is that the religious institutions that are supposed to promote morality has not only compromised it but has had no fresh comment on the subject. The church has obviously held its ground on the matter generally speaking, but in particular the standard has been breached with its leaders as well as with its participants. No one has been able to comment beyond apologies and excuses.

Failing marriages in the church have reached a staggering 50-55 %, and there is no real solution in sight. Some of our most gifted preachers have given a watered down, society pressured responses for this dilemma. The dam has broken, the water is gushing toward us and everyone is denying the inevitable. We are in big trouble down stream, yet the compromise continues.

But God has spoken with great intensity into my spirit concerning the most crucial area of sinfulness in this generation, whether religious or not. He's sent a divine revelation that will resurrect that which is dead and gone in our lives. A revelation that will give our children an example of family: a husband and a wife living in harmony. He has sent a revelation of hope for those who have given up hope. A revelation that will save us from our single-mindedness and self-centeredness, a revelation that will clean us up so that we can be ready when Jesus comes.

So yeah, it's gutsy and controversial and it might be misinterpreted by some, but if a few young people can be persuaded not to go down the ugly path of disappointment I traveled on, it will be worth it. If it stops one young person from giving up their most precious asset, which is their body, it will be worth it. If one young man avoids HIV or one young lady avoids a child out of wedlock, it will without question be worth it!

Introduction

    I will never forget, as long as I live, that Sunday afternoon in May of '96. Little did I know at the time how indelibly important a day it would be, as it pertained to the rest of my life and ministry.

    As I sat on the couch in the living room, wife and child absent, no Sunday afternoon guest or activities to attend to, that afternoon would be like none other. For you see at that time my life was a ball of tension and turmoil. My mother had died less than a year earlier, my stepdaughter from my previous marriage, was fighting off death and depression which attacked her so viciously via an incurable illness and the surroundings of the hospital she was in. And finally, my marriage of four years had deteriorated into a mirage, a mere figment of my most optimistic imagination. As I sat that beautiful Sunday afternoon (beautiful because I was alone and there was no one to upset the atmosphere) I was determined to get a better understanding of this life I was living. I desired an uninterrupted conversation, no better yet, a standoff with God. No television, no music, no food, nothing except me in my apartment staring at the invisible. Demanding, however inappropriately, an explanation from God of why this and so many other relationships I knew of had gone madly off course.

    At first, the quiet seemed noisy. My mind was

extremely cluttered and laden with the luggage of my past and my present. It took time to get free mentally...I mean really free! Then the silence became refreshing and the standoff ended. God is truly amazing, his patience and love is astounding, and his way of communicating is like none other. I can barely pen this page without the tears flowing just remembering how I felt. It was as if God was giving little old me a break, as if I was actually a part of His agenda. I sensed that He wanted me to know that I was not loosing my mind, but rather that He had some peculiar information to share with me to help me understand what I was going through. How gracious He was to me that beautiful Sunday afternoon.

He began by saying to me, "I'm going to show you something that very few people understand. Watch closely as I develop this right before your mind's eye. When I finish, it will all make sense. Sex, marriage, adultery, fornication, relationships, all of it will be made clear to you. And when you share this revelation, it will deliver people everywhere!"

From that afternoon until deep into the night, even when my wife and stepson came home, I was transfixed spiritually and mentally with the monologue God was whispering in my ear. Late that night I can remember not wanting to go to sleep having this slight tremor on the inside, knowing that God himself was speaking with me, and I didn't want him to stop.

I preached part of this revelation in its simplicity weeks later and I knew there was something about this message that would go beyond a sermon on Sunday. This was meant for the masses.

It has taken some time to get to the point of organizing my thoughts and putting this powerful revelation on paper, but I believe you are reading it at the right time to set a new standard for sex, marriage, dating and relationships in your life and for your generation. For in fact, this is a new standard for a new day.

2 Peter 3: 8 says, "Don't be ignorant brethren a day with the Lord is as a thousand years and a thousand years is as one day. The year 2001 represented on earth the beginning of a new millennium, but in heaven it is the beginning of a new day, Day 3 since Christ. I believe Day 3 has always been important to God in the past and will be as important in the future. There are so many Day 3's in the Bible that are significant, that it is safe to say that God often reveals himself or his will on that day or in that number. Moses was hid for 3 months, Joshua prepares the people for 3 days to pass over Jordan, Esther asked the Hebrews to fast for 3 days, Jonah was in the belly of a great fish for 3 days, 3 Hebrew boys were tossed into the fiery furnace, Daniel prays for 3 weeks, Jesus feeds the four thousand after 3 days of teaching, Peter, James and John are considered the 3 of Jesus' inner circle, and the most powerful of them all is Jesus' resurrection on the third day, just to name a few. It is in the dawning of Day 3 that I believe God will reveal many new things to his people; this is just one of them. I pray and know that there will be many more as the Lord prepares his bride for her wedding day.

A Different Era

It was 1969 and I was 8 years old when I accepted Jesus as my savior. I nervously walked down the isle to shake the preacher's hand and give the Lord my heart. I didn't understand all of what I was doing but I knew I wanted to go to heaven when I died.

Being raised in a devout Christian home had a tremendous impact on my life as far back as I can remember. My dad was a deacon in the church. He later became a minister and a chaplain at the prison on Riker's Island in New York City. He preached there every Saturday morning for many years. My mother was a gospel singer. She was the main soloist in the sanctuary choir at the Convent Avenue Baptist Church. I can recall being awakened on Saturday mornings to the hymns of the church being sung by my mother as she did her housework. Sometimes she would hit notes so high that my two younger brothers and me would bury our heads under the pillow to try and cushion our ears. At other times I would hear her singing the songs of the old south and the spirit of God was so strong you'd be nervous to enter the room where she was. I would often catch her wiping the tears away as I turned the corner to see her face.

Every school day morning my mother would have us listening to Family Radio (a Christian broadcast) as we ate breakfast and prepared to go to St. Matthew's Lutheran elementary school, where we received our academic and spiritual training. My dad would pack us up in his checker taxicab and there again we would continue to listen to Family Radio.

It was only when my older brother Daniel went away to college and returned that we were introduced to a new teaching about the Holy Spirit. This was during the beginnings of the charismatic movement. We had been in church all of our lives but we had never understood the Holy Spirit. All we knew was that every once in a while someone would get "happy" in service on Sunday morning and end up falling out under the pew. But when we heard this teaching on the Holy Spirit, though I was just a young teenager, I knew something different was taking place in the spiritual life of my family. We were no longer just going to church, we now understood that "we are the church."

It was around this time that my brother Daniel became the pastor of a small tradition Baptist church and I began to transition away from the church of our upbringing and venture to join with him for Sunday morning services on my own. To this day I don't really know what made me want to be with him in that church, but I know now it was God preparing me for ministry.

Soon I became his right hand man. I was there whenever and wherever he needed me. Today we call it an armour bearer; back then I just called it helping and supporting my brother in any way that I could. I began to see ministry from a different perspective and soon understood the responsibility and the weight of it all.

One of the old preachers at the church watched me closely and noticed my commitment to the church and the next thing I knew he asked me to become the church janitor. I went from there to being an usher, then to singing on the young people's choir, and then to serving as a trustee.

It was around this time that my mother and father

began attending Pentecostal and Charismatic ministries in and around the city. We would go to the Tabernacle of Prayer in Jamaica, N.Y. to hear Apostle Johnnie Washington preach, or to Abundant Life Tabernacle to hear Apostle Jasper Rolle, Jr. preach. We also visited the home of Clinton and Sarah Utterbach when they were just starting the Redeeming Love church, or we would travel out to Coudersport, P.A. to hear the prophetic voice of Pastor David Minor, just to name a few. Additionally, my brother Daniel would invite people like Evangelist Jackie McCullough and Prophet Brian Mosley to do revivals at our church and this was unheard of at that time for a Baptist church.

During this same time period God spoke to my mother to start a Bible study in our apartment and she began to teach on the Holy Spirit, the gifts of the Spirit and other key doctrines that we where being exposed to. People would come from every where to that little apartment in the Bronx and get filled with the Holy Spirit and healed or delivered on Monday nights at "Mother Byrd's" Bible study.

I was now in my late teens, I was near graduating from high school and my desire was to be a professional basketball player but my mother kept telling me that God had a call on my life. I would tell her all the time that I was content helping my brother in ministry and I had no desire to be a minister. She would tell me that I needed to be baptized with the power of the Holy Spirit and I would tell myself that the Spirit of God was already in me. I did my best to fight it, but I lost.

In 1978 God started speaking to me about preaching the gospel. That year my mother and some of the saints prayed with me to receive the baptism of the Holy Spirit and I received and by February of 1979 I preached my initial sermon and entered the ministry. I began working on Wall Street, attending the New York School of the Bible and preaching all in the same year.

After being in ministry 7 years, God focused the call on my ministry in the area of evangelism. At 26 years of age I started the Jesus Makes the Difference Ministries, Inc. We were a fired-up group of young people that organized crusades all around the New York area and won hundreds if not thousands of people to Christ. It was an amazing era in my life and ministry. We saw people healed and delivered on the spot. Even the churches that opened doors for us were blessed and transformed by this ministry. I will never forget how God moved in our lives and established us even in our immaturity.

However, there was one thing that this era did not give me. It was the only subject that throughout all of my years in the Baptist church, the Lutheran school, the Pentecostal revivals, the Charismatic worship experiences and even the Bible studies at our home, no one ever taught about…the subjects of marriage, sexuality and relationships.

During this era it was still taboo. Sex was hush-hush. Dating and embarking on romantic relationships was a hit or miss, learn-as-you-go undertaking. It was the only area that no one ever said anything about. We understood that the 70's began the era of the sexual revolution. We heard terms like "free love" and "free sex" but were sheltered from really understanding what was going on around us. So in the midst of this notorious era in American history I had no insight, no biblical teaching and no training on how to manage romance as a young minister in a leadership position, with great responsibility. With all that I had going for me I did not have an understanding about the one area that could really crucify me in the long run.

But today we are living in a different era. We can no longer afford to ignore the obvious. The ignorance of the past has led us to a place of severe consequences and reper-cussions. We can no longer pass out condoms to our chil-dren and keep our fingers crossed hoping that they can handle what they are about to get themselves into. We can't leave the teaching and training about sexuality to the educational system or to Hollywood. We live in a society that demands tolerance for all types of people with all kinds of views. However, if we are not careful tolerance will lead to acceptance. We must tolerate some views in order to show love and gain understanding from someone that has been tainted or abused in life. Yet I will only accept in my life and in my household what it right and true. This culture has become so manipulated by tolerance that they are now accepting things they would have rejected ten years ago. Now acceptance when it is fully digested will ultimately become practice. Many believers today are now practicing or allowing the practice of things in their midst that 30 years they would not even tolerate. Amazing!

Peter says in his epistle to be "sober and vigilant" otherwise the adversary will slip right in and water down your standards. The next era must bring clarity and understanding. It must produce standards and character. It must establish truth and purity.

Whether you are a mature adult or teenager, as you read this book keep in mind that you are living in **a different era.** God is expecting us to take responsibility for our children and our generation. We can no longer accept a child reared in a Christian household with all of the spiritual reinforcements around them to end up with children out of wedlock, divorced or caught up in adultery or fornication.

For Jesus sake and for the sake of the church we must address what we refused to talk about in the past.

Where we are...

This is what the Lord says: "Stand at the crossroads and look; ask for the ancient paths, ask where the good way is, and walk in it, and you will find rest for your souls." But you said, "We will not walk in it." Jeremiah 6:16

I remember many years ago hearing a nationally known charismatic bishop preach a message called "Crisis at the Crossroads". He used this text out of the book of Jeremiah and described his dilemma. I mention that because I feel we are at a crossroads again, but not as a church or a cultural group but more so as a generation people who must make some serious decisions for the sake of the coming age.

For the youth that are developing now, sex is not a hush-hush issue. It's in the music videos, it's in just about every television show, it's in the schools, it's on the corners where they hang out, it's on every newsstand, sex, lust and compromise is now an everyday experience. The youth of today are immune to the sacredness and sanctity of the union between a man and a woman. They have not heard of this purity, their parents can't teach it because they don't live it, and there is no place they can go (church included) where they can find a foundation for it. Sure some still accept marriage as a worldly institution (not a God ordained institution) and some want to marry some day. Even the latest statistics state that ninety-five percent of all Americans marry at least once before the age of seventy-five. However, it does not stand as the only context whereby **sex** is to be permitted. So without foundational truth alive in our youth, they experiment with and practice different value systems attempting to find one that they believe will work for their state of consciousness. How dangerous is that?

The results of this crisis do not have to be re-examined. Just look at our present generation of adults of 40 and under. They have become the factual data. Divorce, remarriage, single parent households, children raising children, absent fathers, rape, living together, homosexuality, stepparenthood, poverty, disease, inadequate home education, daycare, foster children and the list goes on, are all the results of the new undefined family. These realities all represent the crisis we have adapted to living with from generation to generation. With these conditions facing us, we must seriously pursue redirection for the sake of our children and generations to come.

We must also consider another facet of this crisis. Consider the fact that most parents and single adults are so preoccupied with self-centered goals and aspirations that they are not interested in leaving a legacy in their children. Neither are the single adults interested in taking on the responsibility of a child that is not their own.

So let's take look at the candidates that are available for marriage. We have the absent father who is either struggling to stay alive or afloat. He is in most cases selfishly motivated to appease himself through pleasure and work. He views time with his child as taking away from those things he'd rather be doing. His accomplishments or lack thereof cause him to create a value system that doesn't include the enhancement of a child's life. He usually has no time for self analysis or redirection to a life centered on family values.

We have the single parent mother who is also preoc-cupied with survival from a different perspective. She has to survive for the sake of her child. This in and of itself becomes a grueling assignment. She also depends on agen-cies as well as relatives to assist in the raising of the child, and in many cases that child is raising itself. Also included in this picture is the relationship between the male child and the mother, which is often distorted. He is called the man of the house, without being taught how to be a man, and with-out an example of what a man should be in the home. He is confused as to how to respond to his mother. One day he is a son, another day he is a protector, another day he is her love and companion.

The relationship between the daughter and the mother is also indistinct. She is confused as to how she and her mother will survive. She needs a father. Her relationship is that of a daughter, but is often quickly changed to girl-friend and advisor. She sees things that she has to adjust to without proper explanation, such as different men in her mother's life, anger, disappointment and resentment. She also has to almost simultaneously work through hormonal and physical changes in her body, while raising herself because mom is working, going to school or dating. Lack of attention can create several different scenarios. She could find a replacement for the lack of fatherly love in an older man who controls her. She could find a younger man to make her feel like the woman she grew up to fast to become. She could move into low self-esteem and indulge in any kind of self-destructive activity. I can recall watching Tupac Shakur's song and video "Brenda's Got a Baby" which is based on a true story. The video tells the whole story. If you get a chance check it out, the harsh reality is displayed poet-ically and pictorially. The summation is that Brenda's deci-sion to have sex and have a baby is a result of a broken household and an absent father.

We have the single female with no children; she has a unique challenge. Do I give up my freedom, my life, my goals, or who I am, to have a relationship? The answer is often, no. Some have totally given up and gone to lesbianism which does not satisfy the maternal instincts, others have decided to become as non-committal as men and simply date here and there and sleep around for pleasure. Those who have strong religious views and practices have decided to focus on spirituality and wait for destiny to run its course.

We have the married couple who has endured so many hardships that they are no longer enjoying marital bliss; it's more like marital bust. But they can't divorce or break up because they can't *afford* to pay for the lawyers or the fees and neither of them really have enough money to make it on their own. Sometimes they stay together for the sake of their children but that often turns out to be more of a disaster for everyone involved. So they drift apart while living together and maintain their own individual worlds often inclusive of other illicit relationships.

We have the on again off again marriage, sometimes they are together and sometimes separated. This only leads to further confusion and eventual permanent break up. The example once again is tragic to anyone that has to follow in his or her footsteps.

We have the couple that is living together to see if they have what it takes to be married one day. This is such a vast group. Everybody's doing this. Some of my most respected friends have resorted to this. It's playing house without the binding contract. It's sampling the milk without buying the cow. Sometimes I don't understand why women put themselves in this predicament. Maybe its desperation or the need for security, I'm not for sure, but it sure makes for an easy way out for the man that says, "That sure was tasty, but now I've got an appetite for something else." Men love the meal but hate the responsibility of having to supply the food. As soon as things get sticky most of them disappear, off to find another yielding female.

Then we have homosexuals. Happy to say, I cannot comment too greatly on this area because I just don't get it. One thing for sure, the loyalty and security here is less than in a heterosexual relationship. I say that because there is no binding marital contract between two men or two women and no children that they can truly take biological responsibility for. For those states, like Hawaii, New York, New Jersey and others that are attempting to make this partnership legal, God knows there is no binding spirituality behind it. I'll make this point crystal clear in the chapter called 'Covered by the Covenant'.

We have single men who refuse to be tied down. They are enjoying this no obligation, no commitment lifestyle so much that it becomes illogical to give it up to be with one woman for the rest of their life. These same men have a list of mangled female lives trailing them that could mark off a hundred yards on a football field twice over!

Well, I could continue the list of 'where we are' but I'm sure you've got the picture. In your own mind and experience you can fill in the rest with where you are and the story will go on. But let's stop here for now, and consider, *where we are headed.*

Where we are Headed...

Moral is defined in Merriam Webster's Collegiate Dictionary as "of or relating to principles of right and wrong in behavior: ethical {~judgements}; expressing or teaching a conception of right behavior."

Now consider if you will the moral climate of those parents who have produced these 'millennium adolescents'. I use the term millennium adolescents to describe those born in the 90's who will become adolescents in the new millennium. For these parents and children, in large part morality either has no definition or a muted definition and this is the initial difficulty. When we think of the overall steady moral decline of the last 80 years we can only realistically expect that the millennium adolescents will maintain this decline if not accelerate it.

While watching an episode of the talk television show called "Maury Povich", he displayed five millennium adolescents who obviously could not spell the word morality, much less know the meaning of the word. They had absolutely no respect for themselves or anyone else. They were all raised without the presence or participation of a loving father and they were all sexually active in the most graphic ways. These young girls were resistant and outrageous. In all of their defiance, their sexual conduct was most appalling, especially because they were so young and ignorant of what they were setting themselves up for. They were uneducated to the fact that the habits of their adolescence would have serious repercussions in their posterity.

I looked at this as a perfect example of where we are headed morally. If we are willing to parade our youth on the television screens of America and glorify to some degree the level of decline of our **own** children, then where will morality find its footing. Will morality be reborn on its own? How can these poor children initiate something they have no reference of? Should we even expect a return of morality? Certainly, the viewers young and old will only imitate what they see and feel hopeless about where we are headed.

Our present direction is largely predictable. Taking a good look at these young ladies only reinforces the tragedy of broken marriages, unwed mothers, uncommitted fathers and free sex.

Children born in the last ten years are going to be facing serious sexuality and relationship decisions in the next ten years. (If they are not already facing them) The questions in large part will be the same as the ones of generations past. When should I have sex? How do I know when I'm in love? Who should I marry? Am I gay? Should I have this baby? Should I get a divorce? Why did I marry so young? The difference will be the information they will be using to come to their conclusions.

Psychologists have already proven that the greatest influences on a child's decision making process are their parents or the household they are raised in. With that in mind, think of the homes these children are coming out of. Sixty-seven percent come from single parent households. Women largely manage these households. This automatically means that day care, relatives, afterschool, babysitters, television, and peers are raising these children. None of these avenues necessitate standard bearers. This means that in large part this next group of children will soon enter adolescence with no real assistance or guidance, so *their* decisions will simply be...**theirs!**

After a look at morality we must take look at its mirrored image which is spirituality. Presently, I've noticed that my generation is barely attending any type of worship experience with any regularity. At best we are talking maybe once a month. So our children will copy our habits with only a percentage of the loyalty and conviction we display (if at all). In addition the church has two major problems. The first problem is that from the pulpit to the door of most churches, the institution is plagued with the same lowered standards of sexual morality as are found outside of the church. The lewdness has swept through and consumed the masses just beyond the stained glass windows and right below the crucifix. Divorce is common place, homosexuality is in many cases accepted as an 'alternative' lifestyle, and living together is a justifiable prerequisite to marriage.

The second major problem we face is that the only theology taught about sex in the church is the equivalent to the slogan, "just say no!" Other than that there is no conscious, definitive, intentional theology being taught to help us understand and digest God's standard about sex, marriage and the male/female relationship.

If no one is setting any spiritual or moral standard and many older folks are scared of having their skeletons in the closet exposed, what does that leave for the next group coming along after us? Well you can see the answer to that question everyday at the shopping mall or at the club or in the corridors of most elementary and high schools. The little girls are looking more and more like women. The make-up is going on earlier. The outfits are tighter and more provocative. The pressure for sex is starting earlier. And the guys are more brazen and less responsible.

We also have to reckon with the fact that the millennium adolescents are not loyal to anything or anybody that can't give an answer to the questions "why or why not?" They are looking for sensible answers that most adults aren't equipped to handle. So if you can't give them a sufficient response to their question, they will disregard your advice and engage in their own practices.

So in order for our theology to properly counter the pressure of this generation, it's got to have the facts straight and the answers irrefutable. This poses a problem for ninety percent of the pulpits in our country regardless of the religion.

In light of these disparaging acknowledgments we must face the inevitable. Most of our children will be living by their own rules. The decision to engage in sexual activity will be based on the next raunchy music video or maybe good old peer pressure, since 'everybody' is doing it. Or maybe the decision will be based on curiosity; I wonder what it feels like? Maybe they will regard the fact that mommy has had four men in her bedroom in the past year. Or the fact that the musician at my church is a homosexual so it must be okay to be gay. Maybe their decision will be justified because the pastor has a girlfriend and a wife. Maybe they will be influenced because he or she said they love me and that makes me ready for sex.

Then there is still the off chance that some will abstain because they have other pursuits and dreams and sex is not so prevalent in their minds.

Are we headed toward more cases of HIV and STD's? Are we headed towards more children born out of wedlock? Are we headed towards more children growing up angry, resentful and rebellious because their daddy is AWOL (absent with out leave)? Are we headed towards 'love being the basis for a family' rather than a husband and a wife? Are we headed towards more abusive stepfathers and families where the siblings are only partly related? Yes, I'm afraid we are headed towards certain disaster!

Unless...unless we redirect this generation toward

some basic or traditional guidelines designed not to harm us or eliminate pleasure, but to preserve us and sustain the enjoyment of the male/female relationship. As you read on remain open to the redirection of your notions about marriage, sexuality, dating, and relationships for this new millenium.

In His Eyes or In His Heart?

...He who finds a wife finds a good thing, and obtains favor from the Lord...Proverbs 18:22

The searching process is as important if not more important than the marriage. Simply put if the search is tainted the marriage will be tarnished. I believe that God is so concerned with protecting a woman from the wrong man that the dating process puts him under greater scrutiny than the woman.

Just as giving it a year is important for both parties; it can also serve as a time for the woman to discern whether the man is after what he sees with his eyes or what he knows in his heart.

Notice the Proverbs passage says, 'He who finds a wife' and not 'she who finds a husband'. I don't think that this should be taken for granted. There is a reason why he is searching and she is not. It's certainly not the fact that the woman will not be physically attracted to the man of her dreams or have an idea of what she's looking for in a man. Neither is it that she doesn't have the ability to seek and choose wisely. But more importantly, God is protecting her from being vulnerable in the process. A woman that pursues a man is normally viewed as being easy. Knowing that the man is a hunter by nature searching and pursuing only what he **really** wants, if a search is not necessary he will take what is available whether he wants it or not. This is why the woman becomes vulnerable. If a relationship is initiated based on her pursuit, she can not be sure that she has won the attention of the man because his heart is involved or because he likes what he sees and it is easily attainable.

This is why playing 'hard to get' is not the worst thing for the woman to do. It grants her the opportunity first to discern whether or not he is pursuing her for a night or a lifetime. There is a world of difference between the two. Notwithstanding, many women would use this occasion to get a guy to spend money and waste precious time pursuing something he will never acquire. I would certainly discourage that approach. But it is really a two way street. She can observe his intentions and he can observe whether or not there is any real potential for a relationship. Women beware that you do not enjoy the 'wining and dining' so much that you overlook what is really important and that is his heart.

Sometimes the wining, dining, dating and waiting can be so overwhelming that before you realize it you have given him the impression that he is moving towards a serious relationship. This becomes dangerous if you are just enjoying the moment. Along with this scenario comes the problem of being drawn in by a loving action and not a loving heart. Unfortunately nowadays many women are willing to settle for the loving actions, the money and clothes, cards and candy, flowers and phone calls, and what seem to be the characteristics of a loving, giving and caring man. While these factors will allow you to notice that he is in pursuit, you still need to know exactly what he is pursuing. Many women discover that once they have given in to the sexual pressure and relinquished their bodies as the object of his pursuit that shortly after his chase is not the same. More times than not the hunt ends.

God's desire is to protect the woman by giving her

the option to turn down the advances of a man on the hunt because she senses the difference between sensuality and sensitivity, between lust and love. This is why the emotionally based nature of a woman is so important. While a man can *think* he is making progress because of her acceptance of his actions, a woman can *sense* whether his motivation is right or wrong.

Remember, ninety-nine percent of the time a man *sees*, and then he *wants*. He is designed to be moved by the visual first, more than the emotional. This is why in your average shopping mall there are more women's apparel stores than men's apparel stores. Women know that if I look a *certain* way, I get a *certain* look. Most men are driven by a search for a look and a perception of what that look will do for him with her at his side.

But here's the problem. If he's only after what he sees with his eyes and not what he feels in his heart, what will happen when what he sees changes? The reality of every woman's body or presentation is that it will change over a period of time. Even if they are fortunate enough to have cosmetic surgery, their look is bound to change. Most women don't realize until after they are married or too emotionally involved that they were simply the object of his visual and sexual pursuance, rather than the result of the search for the love of his life.

Knowing the difference between lust and love is the key. The question is, does he lust you so bad that he is willing to love you to get what he wants? Or does he love you so much; he will want you when your looks change? Remember when the lust subsides the love may no longer be a guarantee. Women must know how to determine the difference between the craving of the eyes and the need of the heart. The easiest way for a woman to know the difference is to remember, what comes from the heart reaches the heart.

So many things in a relationship will change over time when the object of his pursuit is sex. There is the 'before and after' sex kind of man. Don't fool yourself and wake up after sex only to find yourself confused, depressed and disappointed! Don't allow yourself to enter the sexual relationship without the contract of marriage! Don't permit yourself to be so overwhelmed by the quest of a boyfriend that you forget what you're truly waiting for is *a husband!*

Men find wives by looking for them, whereas women find husbands by recognizing them. The more you know about what you need, the less you will risk just getting what is offered to you. Many times men will pursue what they see so intently that they won't identify what they need until the novelty has worn off. That's when he discovers that the body is suitable but the personality is not. Maybe the face is attractive but the habits are repulsive. She might have eyes that are enchanting but the intelligence is deficient. He may find that the legs are long and lean but the temper is short and the tongue is sharp. The **finding** is as important for him as the **recognition** is for her.

Don't be fooled! There is a big difference between what the eyes see and what the heart feels. Both men and women need to be aware of this long before they say 'I do'.

Most of the pursuits of my past were based completely on what I saw (or thought I saw) and not based on what my heart felt. Actually for me, the pursuit was the most enjoyable part of the relationship. Even after I was aware that they were not the 'one' for me, the need to conquer became the motivation. Men are indeed motivated by an ego that needs a history of victories. Men, sometimes it takes a long time to realize that the victories we need are not that of another woman but rather of a defined purpose, the conquering of our fears, and destiny in God.

Women ask yourself the question, "Am I in his eyes or in his heart?" Then be patient and wait for the answer to be unveiled for you. It may take some time but the answer may be the difference between love for a lifetime or a lifetime of loves.

Give it a Year!

Each young woman's turn came to go in to King Ahasuerus after she had completed twelve months' preparation, according to the regulations for the women, for thus were the days of their preparation apportioned: six months with oil of myrrh, and six months with perfumes and preparations for beautifying women. Esther 2:12

Before a young lady's turn came to go in to King Ahasuerus, she had to complete twelve months of beauty treatments prescribed for the women. This was mandatory; there were no shortcuts for proper preparation.

I read an anonymous proverb somewhere that goes like this, "Western marriages start out on fire and end with barely a spark, while eastern marriages start with a spark and end on fire." Well, I don't know if its still true but gauging from what I've seen in the West I can agree with at least half of the proverb.

There are plenty of cultures in the East that still hold to the tradition that your parents, who know you best, choose your life long mate for you. (From what I've heard and read the divorce rates in these cases are significantly lower than in other cases.) There are some cases in scripture where this practice was meaningful (refer to Genesis 24, 26:34, 35; Look at Esau).

For me being born and raised in the inner city wasn't easy. As previously stated, I had God fearing parents, they reared us in the "fear and admonition of the Lord." The spiritual deposit has proven to be invaluable, however, we lacked training in some of the other crucial areas of life. Growing and maturing by the grace of God has helped me to look back and recognize the imbalance. I don't fault either of my parents (they did the best they could). Yet now I understand how important it is for the father to develop and redirect strong-willed male children to keep them from making mistakes that could easily be avoided.

One thing I was never taught was the importance of time and process in a relationship. I was shouted at and scolded almost out of alarm and fear, but never enlightened even biblically about the significance of time and process.

My early days of dating always led to irresistible feelings of marriage after...well an average of three months. I mean the intensity would build in the first three weeks like an active volcano and psychologically I thought I had to marry as soon as possible. Thank God I didn't have the means to follow through with those foolish thoughts in my early twenties, but Lord knows if I could have, I would have.

My real problem was that I loved the feeling of being in love. Most times I completely overwhelmed the other person to the degree that as long as I was giving they were taking. I focused all of my energies on the feeling of being in love and that became the preoccupation. As a result, only a short period of time elapsed before the mutual feelings of being together all of the time was dominant in both of our psyches. In my mind this was interpreted as a reason to get married. This was so unfortunate because as soon as I had the means I was married. The first time was at the age of 26 and the second at the age of 30.

As I reflect on what preceded both of these marriages, I can see now that they were doomed before they got started. I accept the responsibility in both cases. Not because the wives don't deserve some of the burden, but because I can remember some of the events surrounding the marriages were a byproduct of my being in love with the feeling of love and they became the victims of that emotion. Surely that was the wrong reason to marry.

Regarding the first marriage, I was rebounding from an engagement gone sour to a young lady I was dating for quite some time. She was scared of marriage and I don't think she's married to this day. We were off and on with an engagement for a while before a real attempt was made at getting married. About a month before the date I was having feelings of uncertainty. My brother encouraged me to call it off if I wasn't sure. I had grown to love her but because of time and experience with her I didn't trust her. That apprehension paid off when I found out an ex-boyfriend had been visiting her and maintaining contact on a regular basis. God spared me that misfortune but I did not learn my lesson. I was still in love with the feeling of being in love.

During this time in my life my popularity was at a peak at my home church and the young ladies were only a grab away. Though I had a huge ego at the time, I lacked confidence and didn't really know who I was. I can remember calming down and thinking I needed a nice church girl that would be trustworthy. The next thing I knew, within three or four months, I went back to the high pressure, fall in love yesterday, style of relationships. I was rebounding all over the place and now that I was living alone this presented a totally differently scenario for me. I was not familiar with managing my life on my own, so my quest was for someone to accommodate me. Before I knew it, I rebounded into the arms of someone who would do the things I thought I needed.

To complicate living alone I was trying to finance my lifestyle on my own and I wasn't doing a good job. This accentuated my inability to make and manage money without the help of a woman. This is another issue men must reconcile within themselves. Too often marriage means two incomes, more money and shared expenses. I did not view the financial welfare of the homes as my exclusive responsibility. When I contemplated marriage I always considered the financial benefit. Instead of taking the time to look in the mirror at myself and make changes I would rather loose myself in a relationship and ignore this basic foundational issue that every mature man should address. Well, I wasn't mature at that point, and I was missing those important ingredients.

Last and most frightening, I never asked her to marry me. Marriage became the assumption as it had in the past. It was only based on being around each other all the time and building this intense psychological and emotional dependency. I did not take the time to build up to the big question. I admire the cultures that insist upon this, especially when you have to ask the father for the women's hand in marriage. We should go back to that. Instead for me, it was three months of being in each other's face every chance we got until the assumption became "let's get married" not "will you marry me?" From that came a flurry of events that led to a ceremony, much of which represented seizing the moment more than anything else. The whole thing took less than a year or actually closer to nine or ten months.

In the first year the realization of how superficial the relationship was, wasn't very obvious. We had good friends around us and I forged ahead as an evangelist with determination and persistence. But I knew that it was not the bond of marriage that kept me with her. If I had given the premarital relationship at least a year I know that I would not have gotten married at that time. The four seasons of getting to know someone are crucial. Things will come out that sober you up and dispel the infatuation.

By year two, with very little true happiness, but

mostly tolerance working in my favor, someone happened into my life. In an instant of meeting her I knew I had certainly made a mistake with the prior choice to be married. I would say to myself, "if only I had taken my time and not rushed into this marriage, I would be free and single right now." My heart changed toward my wife, the relationship floundered and ended in divorce a year after separation.

Marriage two was on the heels of the divorce of marriage one. The key facts were similar, well almost exactly the same. The difference in marriage two was that I knew her since we were teenagers. We tried to date unsuccessfully then but we attended the same church so we saw each other a lot through that medium, however, our lives went separate ways for many years. She married and had a child and I had no interaction or friendship with her for almost ten years.

When we embarked on new relationship as adults, I assumed I knew her. That was a monumental error on my part. Knowing her as a teenager and then as an adult was as different as knowing the night from the day. And as with the first marriage, I was rebounding. Not only from marriage, but from several intense short-term relationships tainted with the same psychological pressure that made me think marriage or at least "be together" day in and day out. The last two short-termers overlapped mentally. My focus would shift to the new person I met and I would work towards maneuvering out of the old relationship. In reality nothing had changed. The divorce had traumatized me. My ego was truly devastated, but the young ladies didn't know it or didn't recognize it. They were lined up and ready for their day in the spotlight of a young, dynamic, and ambitious minister. However, as a result of the divorce my ministry took a blow and I thought it would never recover.

Still each relationship bordered on the next until I found what I thought was someone that knew me. I thought this would be safe. Was money an issue? Yes, to some degree, it always was. I was living at home again at 29 almost 30 years old. I was back in the ghetto wanting to get out and I saw the easiest ticket as being paid for by two people. Marriage was a viable option.

Again, as with the first marriage, I mysteriously never asked her to "marry me." I remember the day I had planned to ask her. That evening was the first time I recall us having an argument and the proposal never came out. As a matter of fact I remember telling her after the incident that my intentions were to "pop the question" that evening. So marriage again became an assumption of "let's get married" rather than "will you marry me?" As a matter of fact, I was so unsure of my decision that I was embarrassed to tell my family. Once again, this all took place in less than a year's time.

Within six months I knew I had made a huge mistake, all because I made an assumption about knowing her. If only I had taken the first year just to *get* to know her or anyone for that matter I could have spared my life and the lives of those women and their children. If I had taken the time to develop a relationship without the pressure of being in love, having sex or getting engaged the results would have been different. I did not value just getting to know them and allowing them to know me.

So when you look at the second chapter of Esther it pays to notice how the king recognizes Esther and then chooses her. What I did not practice in my life nor did I understand was "the process." The process is necessary. It represents the stages I must go through as a man to make a good choice. Learning to do more than just *look* at women was crucial. Seeing beautiful women daily on the subway, on the job, in the street, was not the issue. What was and is important is recognition. Who are they? From whence do they come? As with Adam upon seeing Eve, these must be the matters of concern and priority. When I read Dr.

Dobson's classic "Love for a Lifetime," I was eternally touched by the process he describes that so many of us negate (men especially).

It takes time to build a foundation from which a relationship can be constructed. Without it, the relationship will surely collapse. Today I can truly say that I have grown to respect this *ritual*. Before I married my wife Maria, I watched the calendar and released myself of the pressure that said, "I must make a decision right now." Esther 2:12 insists upon the process and preparation. After the king chose her, she went through six months with myrrh and six months with sweet odours or perfumes just to make ready for marriage. How glamorous and feminine a feeling to know that your preparation for marriage is so particular and peculiar, so intimate and so discreet.

If only I had known this is the way it should be, life would have made sense, the pressure would have been relieved and I would have been at ease. But manhood has to be established, confidence must be instilled, and maturity attained in order to recognize the necessity of the process.

Now I share with other pre-married couples that I have the opportunity to counsel about the importance of that initial year of getting to know one another and then another year in preparation for the marriage.

Give it at least a year young people, adults, divorcees, whatever the category you fall into, **give it a year**. The four seasons will uncover what you need to discover. Throughout the year there are different emotions that surface for some people at different times. Winter may bring out a difference in personality as opposed to summer. Holidays may revive certain memories. Maybe a loved one died at a certain time of the year or a divorce at another time, or a family related tragedy or loss. In that year's time you at least give yourself the opportunity to identify the things that only time will reveal. You may observe their growth and development or how they handle problems and dilemmas. Don't wait until you are married to find out, when you can enjoy the process that makes known these things beforehand. It may surprise you the difference a year makes, so I say again, *"give it a year!"*

Over-nurtured and Under-developed

When his parents saw him, they were astonished. His mother said to him, "Son, why have you treated us like this? Your father and I have been anxiously searching for you."

Why were you searching for me? He asked. Didn't you know I had to be in my Father's house?"

And Jesus grew in wisdom and stature, and in favor with God and men. Luke 2:48, 49, 52

It is a well-known Judaic tradition that when a child reaches the age of legal maturity they become obligated to observe all the commandments. The ceremony to mark this occasion is known as a bar mitzvah (for boys) or bat mitzvah (for girls). In traditional Judaism, when a boy reaches the age of 13 he begins to participate in the religious life of the community as an adult. As a part of the bar mitzvah ceremony he is called up in the synagogue to read from the Torah (1st five books of the Bible). This is sign to the community that the child is moving from immaturity to maturity, and from childhood to adulthood. This is a strategic time in the life of the child as they begin to move out of the nurturing stage of their life into the development of accountability stage of their life. Not only do the parents change the way that they deal with the child, but the child begins to view itself differently also. In some Christian circles a similar ceremony called "rites of passage" may be celebrated.

In John 2:4, Notice Jesus' response to his mother, "Woman" not mother (and the Greek does not suggest mother) "What have I to do with thee?" Jesus is making a distinction here that began in the Luke 2 passage. He will maintain his relationship with his mother under this context for the rest of his life. Even at his death on the cross Christ still uses the term 'woman' concerning his mother in John 19:26, 27. He says to John, who we believe was the youngest of the disciples, "behold thy mother." Jesus knew his absence from her life would leave her *uncovered* so he provided a *spiritual covering* for her in the person of his disciple John. Now John will *cover* (be responsible for) her for the rest of her days at his own home. For a male child, if you take away the developer of accountability (the father) and just give him the nurturer (the mother) he will be less likely to develop his accountability upward toward God. The lack of Godly accountability will breed a man that will look to lay blame on a woman when things go wrong in his life.

This knowledge is insightful as we look again at Luke's writing in chapter 2, concerning Jesus' childhood. None of the other gospel writers cover this event in the life of Christ. Luke may have investigated this specifically because the tradition of a bar mitzvah had commenced in Jewish life within his generation. So this brief glimpse of Jesus at the age of 12 or 13 allows us to see him as he makes the transition from motherly nurturing to fatherly development and accountability.

This is why the devil works so hard to destroy homes and remove men from the family structure. It takes away the opportunity for the male child in particular, to make the mental and emotional transition that causes him to look away from nurturing and a prolonged obligation to a woman, toward the developmental accountability of a man and obligation to God.

Notice in the above passage that Jesus' mother does all of the talking. "Son, your father and I have been looking for you!" Mary is used to handling him. She has had that major responsibility since he was born. While on the other hand, his earthly father Joseph has been preoccupied with the carpentry business for most of these years. However, things are about to change.

Jesus' response seems to have a tone in it that is not at all child-like. "Why were you searching for me?" Almost as if to say, "I'm not a child (kid) anymore, I can handle myself." I believe this is the sign of the turning point in the life of Christ that transfers him out of the care and comfort of his mother's arms into the command and challenge of his Father's hands. He no longer feels compelled to be shadowed under his mother's wing. His "momma's boy" days are over!

There are times when I find myself cringing when someone categorizes a young man (or an older man for that matter) as a "momma's boy." I realize that term may suggest an endearment more than anything else, however, for me it represents a man that has not moved beyond the codependence and need for the comfort that a mother supplies for a child. If a young man continues to need this type of nurturing beyond his adolescent years it will cause problems when he moves into a romantic relationship with a woman. He will have become conditioned to thinking that the foundation for this relationship is based upon what she can supply for him. Thus, making his life more comfortable.

Women have been designed with the innate ability to nurture anything and anyone. This is essential to child rearing. The loving, patient, self-sacrificing nature of a woman provides a growing child with the type of environment necessary during years when they can't do for themselves. In this same context the woman's nature doesn't change because the child is no longer a child, she still wants to provide these comforts although the child may be at the age where they should be somewhat self-sufficient.

In today's culture this may be more prevalent with men than with women. Presently, women have overcome major obstacles to become less reliant on others. Unfortunately, it is to the degree that many women have decided to do without a man in their life completely. Sometimes they will tolerate one out of convenience, but for the most part he is not really needed. This tends to develop out of resentment from the continuous disappointments they have endured from men that have failed them historically.

To the contrary, with men this plays out in a completely different scenario. Let's refer back to the passage in Luke 2 where Jesus responds to his mother's concerns for him. His reply confirms two things in particular. Firstly, he is initiating the disconnection from the adolescent nurturing stage of his life and secondly, he has to begin to develop, mature and become accountable to what his 'Abba' or Father has purposed for him to do. This is vital to his manhood. Most men don't get to this stage until they are in their late 20's or early 30's. Men are typically just interested in entertainment, fun, and being taken care of until life really hits home. However, Jesus began this process at a very young age with particular emphasis put on his obligation to *his 'Abba'*. He is no longer obligated to his mother; and he is subject to his earthly father, but he is indebted to his Abba. He is the one who will develop his accountability, establish his manhood, and define his purpose.

Throughout the rest of his life and ministry Jesus will have an affinity to his Abba. Every gospel writer will pick up on it. It will not only become the central theme of all that he does, but it will also (according to the gospel of John chapter 6) be the very thing that gets him killed. Jesus knows that he comes from Abba and Abba has the plan for his life. Abba will train him, develop him, challenge him, direct him, authorize him, and push him, all the while loving him with a tough abiding love.

Not only does Jesus recognize the importance of this transition, Luke 2:52 says that he had to grow in four distinct areas to support this purpose. He grew intellectually, physically, spiritually, and socially. This growth and development must be deliberate in all of these areas if real success will be achieved in the area of his purpose. So the maturation process only begins at the point where the adolescent nurturing ends.

Take a moment and think to yourself, how many men do you know that meets these criteria of masculine development and accountability? As a matter of fact, the men we are producing today are not expected to meet this kind of demand because we don't look at men from this perspective anymore. The kinds of men we produce today need a woman to help them define and affirm who they are. How many of our boys' do we expect will begin to walk in divine purpose at 13 years of age? How many of our boys today will shun entertainment and fun, to focus on their foundation and their future. If the answer is almost none, that means we are nurturing them too long.

Consequently, men young and old enter into relationships with women offering and looking for the wrong things. Men often offer a package of good looks, fun times, and enjoying the moment. Nothing long-term and lasting or of any real substance. Then for reciprocation men are looking for love, support, hard work, and all their carnal needs to be met. If these things aren't taken care of it creates difficulty for him. As a result of this, there is a growing divide between men and women. It is defined by less compatibility and association and more frustration mixed with misinterpretation. Women are becoming more developed and focused on what they want out of life, while men are over nurtured and becoming less resolute and significant in the family and in society.

It is time to cut the apron strings and let the boys go! The preeminence of fatherhood must be acknowledged again. If the great divide between the genders will ever be reconciled it's going to begin with a reestablishment of the need for nurturing linked with the importance of accountability and development.

As Jesus made this shift, I believe he moved out of needing from the world, into giving to the world. He could have never offered his life if he was thinking that the world owed him something. Instead, he offers his life because the world needed what he had to give. When you're being nurtured you are in continual need, when you're being developed and made accountable you are being fashioned to give.

The Driver's Seat

I do a lot of driving. I've driven almost everyday for over 10 years to Wall Street from Connecticut. I've put many miles on my car. Most of it has been highway driving during rush hour. When you're behind the wheel as much as I am you do a lot of observing of other drivers. It's almost second nature for me to check out who is in the next lane and get a sense of their driving ability.

For the past two or three years I've been doing my own little survey. Most times by rear observation I try to guess whether there is a man or woman behind the wheel of the car in front of me. Now I know you're thinking, he's going to attack women drivers, but hang on a sec while I explain. What I really try to survey is this. If there is a man and a woman in the car, in what percentage of cases are the men in the passenger seat and the women in the driver's seat?

I've been doing this for quite some time and I've found that 75-80% of the time regardless of age or culture the woman is in the driver's seat. Now it's not so much that she is driving that concerns me, it's that he isn't. And the question I raise is, "why not?"

Why is it that the man is always willing to sit back, relax, and enjoy the ride? Why is it that he is so willing to relinquish responsibility to the woman in his life? Why is it that he doesn't take the initiative to be the one on whom the onus lies? Oh, I'm sure you think I'm getting carried away but keep reading I can get worse.

My concern for men extends beyond driving the car; it's in their lifestyles overall. It is so often that the woman is willing to step up and take the position of responsibility while the man slouches down in his seat and dreamily watches the scenery go by.

I pride myself in being an excellent and professional driver, partly because I watched my dad closely for many years; he was a New York City taxi driver. I also drove limousine for a few years in my twenties. I know what it takes to negotiate the road, avoid accidents and drive defensively. I've managed to it for over quarter million miles without incident. Surely that's not easy feat in the New York metropolitan area.

There are times when I can see the fear and intimidation in a woman's eyes, especially when they are driving a large SUV. They are extra careful and extra cautious. Not that anything is wrong with that but sometimes it creates problems for the other drivers around them. I often wonder how they would respond when confronted with extreme danger on the road. We would all agree driving does not warrant emotionally triggered responses. You must function out of knowing what to do more than anything else.

Well, back to the man. I see him there avoiding responsibility. Driving is not just defined by the act but also by the responsibility. Therefore, the man should be responsible for her protection, for the protection of his children, for the preservation of the car and the lives of others. I wish that men would see it this way. The woman in my life should feel completely confident that she is in good hands and has nothing to worry about.

The greatest compliment I would get from my ex-wife was when she got in the car and within ten or fifteen minutes, she had fallen asleep. What she was saying non-verbally was that she felt completely safe and protected.

Men have to get back to the place of setting the standard by taking responsibility and ownership. Even if we do not feel confident in an area, it's up to us to investigate enough to show an effort and then set a standard based on knowledge if not expertise.

Now women, if he doesn't want the responsibility and challenge that goes with being in the driver's seat, you should not to want him. It's time to stop settling for men that feel like they are men because they have you running around picking up all the pieces they have dropped (partly because they blame you for dropping them). You should want a man who can face the music and own up for his failures. You should want a man that says, "I got it, Baby."

God honors a man that does what Adam didn't do. Adam passed the blame on to "the woman you gave me." (Gen. 3:12) Nonetheless God expects the man to be in the driver's seat, at the controls, negotiating safe passage and taking ownership because he's doing the driving. Besides, the more you drive the better you get at it. The more you take responsibility, the less burdensome it feels. The man that owns the company doesn't awake in the morning feeling I hate my job. His perspective as the owner goes beyond the feelings of the day. Over time it doesn't feel like a responsibility but rather an obligation. I believe women today would really prefer it that way.

I've even noticed in the music over the last ten years that the rappers, the singers, and the ladies are declaring things like *"Bills, bills, bills"* or *"I used to love him"* suggests they are not going to accept men any old way. They are tired of sorry, trifling, uncommitted, unprotecting men for whom they have to provide. They are expecting more than that now, and they should.

The nineties have come to a close and hopefully the

90's women mentality was left behind with those years. Women are not equipped for everything. Let the man take charge. It's time for the woman to sit back, relax and enjoy the ride! Though women have been forced to handle most everything because of unreliable men, women can't do it all. Doing it all will eventually take its toll. Emotionally, physically and spiritually it is draining. Along with the new millennium should come a new generation, a new era, and a new improved set of paradigms.

Gentlemen start your engines!

The Head and The Heart

Who can find a virtuous wife? For her worth is far above rubies. The heart of her husband safely trusts her; so he will have no lack of gain... Proverbs 31:10, 11

Which is more valuable to the human's existence, the head or the heart? Which would you prefer: to be brain dead and have a healthy heart or to have a healthy functioning brain and have your heart stop working? Before you answer consider these two facts about the human body. The heart beats because it receives instructions from the brain. These impulses keep it functioning on a smooth and steady rhythm. Mutually the heart supplies a steady stream of oxygenated fuel to the brain. Without this oxygenated fuel better known as blood the brain would faint, and if it lacked this blood for more than several minutes it would not recover from the loss. Take a moment now and weigh these two options before you deliver your verdict.

The truth of the matter is neither is of greater or lesser importance because each one is dependent on the other. The head and the heart play mutually important roles as it pertains to the well being of the body. As Apostle Paul refers to the man as the head, I would like to refer to the woman as the heart. This reference will allow me to make comparisons of the male/female relationship with greater clarity and significance.

While many have misinterpreted the 'head' terminology as solely a position of power, authority or control, it
in fact can be better described as a position of responsibility,
purpose and vision. It has to be informed, equipped and
continually educated to maintain a consistent pattern of reli-
ability. Part of its ability to carry this out is clearly related to
the fuel that gives it strength and life.

So how did we get so far from a balanced, non-
biased interpretation of the word 'head' in scripture? And
why has so much controversy risen from one scriptural
concept? I have concluded that it is a result of our Greco-
Roman worldview and male dominated society. Most of the
interpretations and definitions we hold to traditionally need
to be re-addressed in light of continuing revelation and
greater enlightenment of God's purposes for the body of
Christ. In times past it was quite easy for men to maintain a
sense of power and domination over women, however God
has allowed women to evolve to a place of recognition and
respect, and we are all better because of it. Notwithstanding,
that the difficulty of the application of this term 'head' still
exist today.

Many have honed in on the passages that use the
context of the head to describe the position of Christ or the
man, and many books have been written on the subject.
Therefore, I will only make a few observations to serve the
purpose of this book.

When we relate the Greek word (kephale) primarily
used throughout the NT for the word head, there are sugges-
tions about the term that are not obvious in the English. The
English language defines it as the upper or anterior division
of the body, which contains the brain, the seat of the intel-
lect, the mind, and even a person with respect to mental
qualities. We tend to translate that into meaning that the
head is the boss. However, the Greek interpretation suggests

(from the root **kapto**) that it could have a military implication. This would mean that the head is the target to be taken hold of or seized as the focal point of the army.

Additionally, the Hebrew word (ro'sh) used for head in the OT, is metaphorically applied to mean leader or person in authority. However, the Hebrew word (ro'sh) is not normally translated to the Greek word *kephale,* a different Greek word like *archon* would be used for this metaphorical meaning. Thus the interpretation of head as in a dominating or controlling figure is not the best context.

The best way to interpret the head as Paul has used it several times in his writings is to balance the context against other scriptures. Ephesians 1:22, 5,23, Colossians 1:18, and 2:10, are a few to consider. Certainly each of the context suggests authority, but they can better be interpreted as responsibility for someone or something. If I am the head of my wife, in reality I am responsible for my wife. If this responsibility is to be taken seriously I must retrieve as much information from her and about her if I am to truly protect and provide for her. Functioning from generalizations about women will prove to be inadequate if my intentions are to meet her specific needs. Additionally, if I am to be the point person for the family, my wife becomes the best source of information from which strategies can be devised and decisions can be made.

From a military perspective the head is in fact the target. Israel was only successful in defeating the Philistines after David conquered Goliath (and decapitated him). Once the leader went down the confidence and moral of the army diminished. The head or the Captain of the armies of Israel gave Joshua the confidence that he would be victorious over Jericho. The head holds the position of great responsibility.

Still the head gets vital information and intelligence from those who are behind the scenes. This is why men must be not good but great listeners. The head may make the decision but the heart fuels it with news, facts and data. This constitutes the balance and the mutual dependency of the head and the heart. With this in mind neither two heads nor two hearts can constitute the same balance. Once again undermining the whole issue of homosexuality.

It is common for us to view anything with two heads as abnormal. Thus in order for two men to get together attempting to redefine the context of marriage, one of them if not both of them must function abnormally. Their roles in the relationship would be overlapping and eventually conflicting yielding chaos. Similarly as with two women the abnormality is defined in being headless and lacking the balance necessary for a truly functional family. As a result chaos would commence with each woman overwhelming the other with news, facts and data and either taking responsibility for the ultimate decision.

If the man is the head, then every head needs a heart. The heart is the compliment necessary for balance. It is fascinating to me that 1 Samuel 16:7 says that man looks on the outward appearance yet God looks at the heart. Perceiving the head is easy but interpreting the heart takes discernment. When I think about the secrecy of the heart, I realize that only the right head can connect to the right heart, discerning and understanding its motivations. As I compare the woman to the heart I see how important it is for each to have distinctive roles in the relationship. The heart not only supplies the head with fuel called blood; it supplies the entire body. Ironically, even when the head is unconscious in sleep, the heart is still quietly pumping away. The heart supplies for the body while the brain provides for the body.

When a woman sincerely takes the responsibility of supplying life-giving blood to the head, she will not be inclined to compete with the head. Knowing that the heart is one of the four vital organs, she will never feel inferior or less important than the head. Still men must redefine their position as it relates to responsibility and the focal point of the attack on the family.

The oneness described in the scriptures can also be likened to the completeness of a man and a woman based on the complimentary workings of the head and the heart. Needless to say the head and the heart hold equal value in regards to the marriage and the wellbeing of the family. As the head I always thank God for Maria, she is my heart.

all heard a loud thud outside that shook the house. Recalls Gibson: "It sounded as though a very heavy solid object such as a safe had fallen from a great height and landed on the bricks of the moat. We rushed outside with flashlights expecting to find something lying there. But nothing unusual was found." This particular manifestation has occurred a number of times over the years, both at night and during the daytime.

The most recent occasion was early in 1985 when a draft copy of the manuscript for this chapter was sent to Gibson for her review. As she sat in the library in the evening to read the script she was startled by what she describes as a "loud KA-WOMP" in the moat area just outside the room. "It was very loud and sounded heavy. I got up to look, but there was nothing there. It was the first time this particular phenomenon had happened in years."

There also have been some sightings of spectral forms. At one in the morning during the summer of 1967, for example, Gibson went into the dark kitchen to get a glass of milk before retiring. From the light shining out from the refrigerator, she caught a glimpse of something in the hall. "I could plainly see the silhouette of a slim girl in a floor-length dress with a full skirt," she says. "It was not the wide fullness of a hoop-skirt, but one from an earlier period. I could see no features, but she was not transparent, just a white silhouette. I saw her for perhaps 10 seconds. In the next instant she was gone. There was no gradual fading away; she simply disappeared from one instant to the next."

One of her daughters had a similar experience several days later. She ran to tell her mother about it, not knowing that her mother had seen a vision, too. The daughter described what she had seen in the drawing room as a "lady in white who was standing in front of the fireplace." She disappeared in front of her eyes.

Gibson later learned that earlier residents of Haw Branch had seen the same apparition. One relative told her that Gibson's great grandmother, Harriet B. Mason, had told of seeing the lady in white, and had once even been awakened from a deep sleep by a touch from the spirit. On other occasions, the McConnaugheys have heard footsteps des-

cending from the second floor to the first.

The very mention of one of her great grandmother's girl-hood friends apparently has been cause enough for other psychic happenings. Lights have gone on and off for no reason when her name came up in conversation. And once, when Gibson spoke of her at the dinner table, two bulbs in the electric chandelier over the dining room table glowed brilliantly and then went out.

There have been unexplained strange odors, also. Several times the strong scent of fresh oranges could be sensed in the library, though there were no fresh oranges in the house, and all frozen orange juice was unopened. Gibson also has smelled an attar of roses when there were no flowers in the house. Another time, Gibson was doing research on the family history at the county clerk's office. She had uncovered some family unpleasantness that involved her great-great-great grandmother and her two daughters' husbands. When the daughters married, their husbands signed a pre-marital agreement that they would never sell the property their wives had been given. But through conniving, the men got control of the good-sized land holdings, and were going to sell them. The great-great-great grandmother sued them, lost in a lower court, but won in an appeals court and regained control of the property for her daughters. Oddly, the next morning after her research, Gibson woke up to a strong aroma of fresh mint.

Aside from the screams, screeches, heavy thumpings, and footsteps, there have been other curious sounds heard at Haw Branch. One of the young McConnaughey sons and several friends, camping out one night in the surviving old slave cabin, heard the sound of a cowbell making a circuit around the building in narrowing circles all night. There are no bells on any of the cows on the plantation!

Other noises center in the attic. All family members at one time or another have reported hearing what sounded like furniture being dragged across the attic floor late at night. Yet when they went up to look, the dust covered furniture was unmoved, nor were there any traces of animals or birds in the attic. Sometimes a rocking chair is heard rocking in the attic, but the chair was broken and no one could sit in it.

On another occasion, a humming sound was heard in the basement. A musician friend of the family said it sounded like an old English folk tune. In the basement, incidentally, there is a sealed room. It is a chamber about four by six feet in size and completely closed off by brick and masonry. The McConnaughey cats seem fascinated by it.

Gibson says there has been a lot of interest in the psychic phenomena in the house and a number of tourists have traveled miles out of their way to visit. Haw Branch was open to the public for some time, but Gibson says it got to be too much for them. "Cary and I are retired now, so the house is no longer open." Several writers have come to the plantation, too, over the years. One was a young woman who was doing a magazine article on haunted houses. She told Gibson she was a skeptic.

"We let her spend the night in one of the upstairs bedrooms to lend authenticity to her article," Gibson recalls with a smile. "Sometime during the night she told me she was awakened by the sound of footsteps approaching her bed. Just then our cat, Fink, shot out of the bedroom. Now fully awake, the woman heard the footsteps come right up to the edge of her bed. She sat up and the sounds ceased. When she turned on the light there was only emptiness in the room. She told me the next morning the experience had made a believer out of her."

But of all the many and varied manifestations of psychic phenomena that have surfaced at Haw Branch, the most intriguing involves the portrait, or rather portraits, for there are two. The first is a large pastel rendering of a young woman named Florence Wright. She was a distant relative by marriage, and little was known of her except that her parents had a summer home in Massachusetts, and that Florence died before the painting was completed, although she was only in her twenties.

After 20 years in storage, the painting was given to the McConnaugheys by a cousin, who told them it was a colored painting. This bewildered Gibson, because, in her words, "when the picture was uncrated and the massive gilt rococo frame and glass painstakingly dusted, the portrait appeared

to be a charcoal rendering, rather than a pastel. No color was evident, everything was either a dirty white, gray or black." There was no signature of the artist to be found, and the back of the frame was tightly sealed. Gibson left it that way and hung the picture over the library fireplace.

A few days later, as Gibson remembers: "I heard women's voices in animated conversation on the first floor of the house. As Haw Branch (then) was open to the public, an occasional group of visitors will walk in without ringing the doorbell, not realizing the house is actually lived in. Calling, 'I'm coming right up,' (I) hurried upstairs from the English basement to find no one there. No car was in the parking lot nor the road leading away from the house. The unexplained sound of voices occurred five or six times in the library over a period of a year."

A few months later Cary McConnaughey was sitting in the library reading a newspaper when he looked up and noticed that the rose in the portrait seemed to have taken on a pink tinge. The girl's black hair also was beginning to lighten, and her grayish skin was turning flesh-colored. These changes continued gradually over the next year until the portrait miraculously transformed into pastel brilliance.

Says Gibson: "A partially opened rose in the portrait began to take on a definite pink cast, when previously it had been grayish-white. Other changes continued gradually for over a year. Several people connected with art departments of neighboring Virginia colleges saw the portrait from the time of its arrival and confirmed the change in coloring, but could offer no logical explanation."

A psychic expert from a neighboring county came over to investigate. He reported that Florence Wright's spirit was tied to the portrait because she died before it was completed, and that she had the power to remove the color from it when she was dissatisfied with where it was placed. She apparently liked Haw Branch, so with help from the spirits of two other young women (allegedly the ones Gibson heard talking in the library), she restored the original color to her portrait.

"Who can say his theory isn't correct," says Gibson. "When the color returned to the portrait and the changes

ended, so did the sound of voices. Today, the girl's clear blue eyes look rather sadly out beneath her curly reddish-brown hair, and her pink and white complexion looks as if she were alive. The green and beige upholstery on the gnome-carved gilt chair she sits in is a deeper shade of the carved jade jar on a table near her. The rose that was first seen to change color slightly is now a clear, soft pink."

In 1971, Gibson wrote, "much about the portrait still remains a mystery. How did the young girl die? Did the partially opened pink rosebud in the crystal vase foretell her early death, or was it added symbolically after she died? Who was the artist, and why did the pastel portrait's coloring change without human assistance? There is a slight lead on the artist's name. When the portrait first arrived at Haw Branch, the owner had told (me) that it was painted by a famous American artist and signed by him, although she couldn't remember his name."

About a year later, some of the answers were learned — in most curious fashion. One summer evening in 1972, one of Gibson's daughters and a friend of hers were sitting on the floor in the library beneath the portrait. They moved over to the sofa, and seconds later the supports of the picture's heavy frame pulled loose. The portrait slowly slid down the wall until the bottom of the frame reached the mantel shelf where it crushed a row of porcelain antiques, tipped forward slightly, slipped over the edge of the mantel and fell to the wide pine floorboards.

As the girls sat transfixed, glass shattered all across the floor. The portrait had fallen face down on the exact spot where the girls had been sitting only minutes before!

"Although the painting itself was undamaged, the big wooden frame was broken," says Gibson. "Lifting it up, we found underneath what had been the tightly sealed backing of the frame, a brass plate that gave the girl's full name, her birth date in Duxbury, Massachusetts, and her date of death in the same place. Though we searched carefully for the artist's signature, both on the front and the back of the painting, it could not be found. The next day, the frame was repaired, the portrait placed back in it and the glass replaced.

The man who did the work searched as carefully as we had searched to find the artist's signature, but with no success.

"It was late in the day when we arrived back at Haw Branch with the portrait. The sun was red and low in the sky. As my husband and I lifted the picture from the back of the station wagon, I happened to tilt my end of the frame slightly upward. Suddenly, as though a red neon sign had been lit, the name 'J. Wells Champney,' appeared. It have been signed in pencil on the apron of the dark mahogany table in the picture. Only under a certain angle of light could it be seen."

The McConnaugheys later learned that the girl in the portrait had been born into a wealthy family that owned several homes. Her parents commissioned Mr. Champney to paint the portrait. Before it could be finished, Florence Wright, who at age 24 was an accomplished musician who had studied piano abroad, slumped over a piano keyboard and died of a massive stroke. The artist completed the painting and added the partially opened rose to signify that his subject died an untimely death before the painting was completed. The McConnaugheys also found out that the artist was later killed when he fell down an elevator shaft in New York City!

Gibson adds that "many say that they can see the girl blush when they stare hard at her portrait. But now that Florence Wright's portrait has regained its original colors and hangs in a permanent home, it seems unlikely that she will ever again change her color, or need her 'spirit helpers.' "

The second portrait concerns a closer relative — Gibson's great-great grandmother — Marianna Elizabeth Tabb, who was born at Haw Branch in 1796 and returned to the home in 1815 as a bride. It was painted by Richmond artist James Warrell about the time of Marianna's marriage to William Jones Barksdale, and hung at Haw Branch for a number of years.

Later, the Barksdales moved to another Tabb plantation home, Clay Hill, where they spent their remaining years. Marianna died in 1856, and on a bitterly cold winter day in January 1861, Clay Hill burned to the ground. The drawing room walls were completely paneled in wood, and portraits

were framed with molding and permanently affixed to the walls. However, during the fire, the portrait of Marianna was saved by cutting it from the molding. What happened to it then is a mystery.

Nearly a century later, in 1948, the Valentine Museum in Richmond had an exhibit of paintings entitled, "Makers of Richmond 1737-1860." A book of the pictures exhibited was published by the museum. Twenty-six years later, in 1974, Gibson McConnaughey saw a copy of the book. In it was a reproduction of Marianna's portrait. But it was listed as the portrait of Jane Craig Stanard, the woman who allegedly was the inspiration for Edgar Allan Poe's famous poem "To Helen."

Gibson knew it was Marianna and not Jane Stanard because in 1860 Thomas Sully had made a copy of the original Warrell portrait, and she had seen this copy at an exhibit at Longwood College in 1973. She wrote a letter to the Valentine Museum telling them of the error in identification. Through correspondence and persistent digging, the museum learned that the Warrell portrait had been bought, possibly sometime in the early 1900s by a Richmond printer named J. H. Whitty. He had, without foundation, identified the young woman in the portrait as Jane Craig Stanard. Whitty was an avid col-

lector of things related to Poe.

Here again, the trail grew cold. Later, the president of the Poe Foundation found that Whitty's collection had been bought by another Poe follower, William H. Koester of Baltimore. Meanwhile, a reproduction of Marianna's portrait was published in a biography of Poe in 1941, again identifying it as the picture of Jane Craig Stanard.

The McConnaugheys, the Poe Foundation and the Valentine Museum kept up their search. When Koester died in 1964, his possessions passed on to his wife and two sons. The address of one of them was located through the Baltimore phone book. Correspondence with him revealed that his father's collection of Poe material had been sold to the University of Texas — with the exception of the Warrell portrait.

Gibson wrote to Koester's son explaining the false identification of the portrait — that it was actually her great-great grandmother and had no connection to Poe. She asked if she could buy or borrow the painting to hang it at Haw Branch. The son replied that his mother wanted to keep it, but that if they ever decided to sell it they would let the McConnaugheys know.

Next, fate played a hand in the odyssey of the portrait. In June 1976, two years after Gibson had corresponded with Koester's son, the McConnaugheys learned, entirely by chance, that the Warrell portrait was to be sold that week at an auction in Baltimore. It was listed as the source inspiration for Poe's "To Helen." The auction house owner was then informed of the portrait's true identity.

At the auction, the portrait was announced only as "a rare old painting by Warrell," although a brochure still described it as linked to Poe. When it came up for sale, Gibson McConnaughey brazenly got up brandishing her proof, and announced to the stunned audience that this actually was the portrait of her great-great grandmother and had absolutely nothing to do with Edgar Allan Poe.

This information precluded the Poe collectors' bidding action and the McConnaugheys were able to purchase it as merely an old painting. They took it home and hung it in the drawing room at Haw Branch. Curiously, since it took its

rightful place in its ancestral home, Gibson says most of the psychic activity at the plantation ceased.

That is the story of the two portraits at Haw Branch. But there is yet a fascinating footnote to the saga; one with spine tingling parallels to the two paintings. Edgar Allan Poe wrote a short story called "The Oval Portrait." In the narrative, Poe tells of a man who spends a night in a strange chateau. He reads late into the night, and in repositioning the candelabrum he sees a portrait hanging on the wall of a beautiful young girl "just ripening into womanhood." He becomes absorbed by the painting which is in an oval frame, "richly gilded and filegreed in Moresque." He describes the portrait as having an "immortal beauty," with life-like characteristics. As Poe phrased it, the man had "found the spell of the picture in an absolute life-likeliness of expression."

In a volume which discussed the paintings in the chateau and their histories, he reads of the background of the portrait. The girl was said to be a "maiden of rarest beauty, and not more lovely than full of glee. . . frolicsome as the young fawn." She fell in love with an artist and married him, but, Poe says, the artist was already married to his career.

He then decided to paint his bride's portrait. She was not pleased about it, but she obeyed, and so, for days and days he painted. He became so absorbed in his work that he did not notice her withering health and spirit. She grew "daily more dispirited and weak," but she continued to sit and smile for she loved her husband-artist so much.

As he neared completion of the portrait, he allowed no one into the turret, for he "had grown wild with the ardor of his work." Rarely turning from the canvas, he did not notice his bride's rapidly deteriorating health. At last he finished, and stood "entranced before the work which he had wrought."

As he admired the canvas, he cried in a loud voice, "This is indeed Life itself!" Then he turned suddenly to his beloved. "She was dead!"

ABOUT THE AUTHOR

L. B. Taylor, Jr. is a native Virginian. He was born in Lynchburg and has a BS degree in Journalism from Florida State University. For 10 years he worked as a writer, editor and public information officer for NASA and NASA contractors at the Kennedy Space Center in Florida, covering every major space flight through the Apollo 11 first manned landing on the moon in 1969. For six years he was editor and publications manager for Rockwell International in Los Angeles and Pittsburgh. Taylor moved to Williamsburg, Va., in 1974 as public relations director of Badische Corporation. He is the author of more than 300 national magazine articles and 28 non-fiction books. His research for the book "Haunted Houses," published in 1983 by Simon and Shuster, stimulated his interest in area psychic phenomena and led to the writing of five regional Virginia ghost books.

L. B. Taylor's Newest Book of Hauntings!!! "Civil War Ghosts of Virginia" 240 pages, illustrated, $12.00. Also Available: "The Ghosts of Virginia, Volume I" — 400+ pages, illustrated, $14; "The Ghosts of Virginia, Volume II" — 400+ pages, illustrated, $14; "The Ghosts of Williamsburg" — 84 pages, illustrated, $6.50; "The Ghosts of Richmond" — 172 pages, illustrated, $10; "The Ghosts of Tidewater" — 232 pages, illustrated, $11; "The Ghosts of Fredericksburg" — 192 pages, illustrated, $10; "The Ghosts of Charlottesville & Lynchburg" — 192 pages, illustrated, $10. Add $3 shipping and handling on single book orders. Add $5 shipping and handling on multiple book orders. Special: All 8 books — $75; All 5 regional books — $40; Virginia Ghosts I & II — $25. Note: If you wish the books signed, please specify to whom. L. B. Taylor, Jr., 248 Archer's Mead, Williamsburg, VA 23185 (804-253-2636).*

Marriage is "A Good Thing"

Marriage is honorable, and the bed undefiled; but fornicators and adulterers God will judge... Hebrews 13:4

Remember Proverbs 18:22 says that marriage is **a good thing** and those who find it obtain the Lord's favor. If marriage is a good thing, and I believe it is, then why do we see so many bad marriages? Why do the statistics about marriage suggest that it is a risky venture? And why do so many people avoid it and just live together? If marriage is not redefined and re-established as a good thing then we will lead the next generation into God's judgement.

Hebrews 13:4 encourages marriage so that you will not be subject to God's judgement. The denial of the goodness of marriage (and sex in this context only) has encouraged fornication by default. So ask yourself the question, "Where did my definition of marriage come from and is it valid?"

For the most part the definition and the establishment of marriage has been taken for granted. It is because of this casual approach that marriage as we know it has been so viciously attacked by liberals and homosexuals. Marriage must be defended by those who honor the One who has established it. However, this defense cannot be taken lightly, it must be clearly defined and established upon a foundation of immutable truth. Since God created and established marriage, we know that we can count on his definition to be reliable and perpetual, transcending time and culture.

In my search for truth and understanding it became obvious to me that a careful analysis of the opening chapters of the book of Genesis would reveal the mind and intent of God, concerning marriage. Careful scrutiny of what is recorded opens us up for continual revelations and insights about relationships, marriage, family, and the original roles of men and women. Some of the insights are simplistic and some are very deep, but they all support the goodness of marriage. I invite you to embark on a journey of discovery that will change your perspective forever.

In the first two chapters of Genesis we seek to discover what is **good** and what is **not good**. In chapter 1 verse 4, on day one God speaks light into existence and notice there is no sun. God calls it **good**. In day two, God does not say it was good, however the scripture says, "it was so". Notice also in day two a "division" was established. In day three there is a "gathering together" and God saw it was **good**. God also establishes a principle that will remain in the earth forever, reproduction from the seed within. Seed being the essence of reproduction. Fruit being the repository or container in which the seed is protected and cultivated. This God saw was **good**. Once again with the "division" noted in verse 14 the sentence ends with "and it was so". Verse 18 describes what rules over the division that He previously created. The lights that are created are the sun and moon and that was **good** also. Next God creates life everywhere, in the waters and above the earth and he sees that it is **good**.

In verses 24 & 25 God speaks into existence things that will creep on the earth and these things are **good**. Finally in verse 31 God examines everything that he has made and it was very **good**. Next in verse 12 of chapter 2 the gold of

Havilah is described as **good**. Eight times in the opening verses of Genesis there is something described as "**good**".

But in chapter 2 verse 18 the term "**not good**" is introduced. In this section of chapter 2 we acknowledge the recounting of the creation story with detail on the creation of Adam, the son of God. (Chap 2:7, see also Luke 3:38) It is at this point that God acknowledges the need for Adam to have a compatible earthly companionship. God's acknowledgement that Adam's loneliness was **not good**, God was implying that the life scenario for Adam was not complete. God's desire for him was made good in the creation of the woman. I also believe that Adam is aware of the fact that all the creatures in Eden are in pairs and he was alone.

God says he will make a suitable helper for him. Verses 19 and 20 describe what God had made and none of these creatures represented a suitable match for Adam. Which means Adam is obviously unique and unlike anything else created up until this point. Notice the end of verse 20 suggests some disappointment on the part of Adam concerning the absence of a comparable companion. It is almost as if God may have revealed to Adam, *"I'm going to create someone suitable for you"*, and then Adam's search comes up empty.

The good thing is Adam recognized what wouldn't work for him. The look, the structure of the bodies, the mental capacity and particularly the inability to communicate with any of these creatures caused him to be convinced they were not suited for him. In order for him to have a suitable helper, he needed to be able to communicate his need to something or someone that would respond in the same language.

Notice in verse 20 "there was not found," which means a search took place. Adam searched and did not find. As a matter of fact during his search he was successful in naming everything that he came across. This restless search may have been the reason why God put him to sleep.

Men still suffer from this same relentless, anxious way of searching for a suitable companion. Day in and day out many of us spend timeless hours in mental and physical pursuit for the woman of our dreams. So everywhere we go we're on the prowl. We often use or mothers or other influential females from our childhood as references. Then there is the Hollywood affect, which infects our psyche. The images from television and in magazines will often have even greater influence, as we grow older. At work, at church, during the commute, at the social event, and everywhere men find themselves the quest never ends. As a matter of fact, it becomes such a part of our nature that even when we find the 'one', we tend to find it difficult to break the habit of being on the hunt.

So God in his wisdom causes Adam to *rest* from his search, causing a deep and anesthetic sleep to come upon him. All of this is a result of God declaring it was "**not good**" for Adam to be alone. God's desire is for Adam to have relationship with a similar yet different person and to establish the context of marriage for Adam's pleasure.

In verse 22 please note Adam does not have to search anymore. Instead God brings the woman to him. At this point all Adam does is recognize the uniqueness of this new creation. He recognizes *similarities* necessary for compatibility. Then he recognizes where she came from. "She came out of me" (he must have recognized the difference in his body; i.e. the missing rib) so therefore she is a part of me. Adam's posture towards the woman is essential to a long-term relationship. If he views her as being a part of himself, he will remain committed to her as he would his own body (see Ephesians 5:28).

Woman, the Hebrew term stated here is "ishshah". It can be compared to "enowsh and iysh", which means man, mortal in a feminine context. This describes what Adam names her. Adam maintains the same posture with this new creation as before; he names what he sees. Unless the man is able to recognize, identify, name, categorize and communicate to her who she is to him, the declaration of *one flesh* can not be substantiated. God's criteria for marriage are wrapped up in verses 23 and 24. This obviously is God's definition because He uses a context that is not yet understood (it doesn't exist before now) to the man and the woman. He uses the term father and mother. This would be obscure to Adam and his wife; therefore we know it is God's creation and definition.

I've heard the cliché "leave, weave and cleave" used to describe the meaning of verse 24. Now that Adam is not alone and God's definition for marriage is established, we can safely say this now constitutes a "**good thing**." They are also totally exposed to one another yet unashamed. Seemingly vulnerable, but in fact completely and uniquely designed for one another. They have the ability to communicate distinctly and differently than with any other creature, thus creating an extraordinary bond. A husband and wife should have their own unspoken language, a way of communicating that only they understand. Ideally this would make them impenetrable. This was a "**good thing**".

So now I am challenged but comforted because my issues surrounding my difficulty and disappointment with marriage are beginning to be resolved. My question that Sunday afternoon born out of frustration and societal pressure was "Are we made to co-exist?" Does Mars and Venus, get along? If Christian marriages are failing just like non-Christian marriages, where then does the answer lie? My frustration began to dissipate as I began to see for myself how God's plan for men and women does in fact make sense. So it is a **good thing** to be married!

Now I can rest. However, I realize most men will not stop the relentless search and let God bring the suitable woman to them. We are created to pursue and conquer and it will be difficult to redirect that nature when it comes to our search for the right woman. Men must accept the responsibility of knowing the role a woman should play in their lives, and they should be able to identify that upon meeting and getting to know that woman. This would keep men from abusing, exploiting and manipulating the women in their lives.

The easiest way to recognize your wife is to know yourself. If she will be your suitable helper then you have to know your strengths and your weaknesses. Not only know them but also be willing to acknowledge them and share them with the helper God has given you. Maybe you, like myself, had given up on finding the right woman. Well, there is hope in the will of God. Remember it is **not good** for you to be alone; there is a seed of purpose, a seed of creativity, a seed of principle in you. It is to be planted in a suitable vessel to cultivate and nurture it and to bring forth fruit. Therefore, God wants you to be perfectly matched in marriage. Adam and Eve and all creation were blessed to be fruitful and multiply and replenish the earth. This is why homosexuality never was or will ever be an acceptable alternative relationship entity. There is no possibility for the homosexual union to reproduce.

Reproduction is the obvious sign of God's ability and desire to create a heritage and a legacy from a union. It is his way of endorsing the union. It is in this area that God's sovereign will is manifest, however, man is trying everyday to manipulate the process of conception. A human seed can only properly germinate under one condition; it must be deposited in a similar yet different vessel designed to make it more than a seed. Two seeds or givers (men) coming together can not reproduce anything; just as two eggs or vessels (women) coming together can reproduce nothing on their own. Therefore there can be no heritage or legacy produced from those types of relationships, hence no endorsement from God. Refer to Paul's writing to the Roman church in chapter 1:26, 27.

Because of this, God gave them over to shameful lusts. Even their women exchanged natural relations for unnatural ones. In the same way the men also abandoned natural relations with women and were inflamed with indecent acts with other men, and received in themselves the due penalty for their perversions. (New International Version)

I encourage you men, especially those who have never been married, to rest and wait for God to bring her to you, that way you will be guaranteed not a perfect person but a perfect match. Invest your time in getting to know yourself. Stay in tune with the spirit of God, your maker, and you will be able to discern who's standing in front of you.

Remind yourself of the goodness of marriage. It's not that being single is a curse, however because of the negative connotation of marriage we must be aggressive to declare that marriage is a **"good thing!"**

Adam, Eve and God

So now that my hope has been restored in the perfection of God's marriage institution, deeper revelation has begun to unfold. My understanding about men and God's covenant, and women in light of that covenant had been very limited in regards to marriage. But I questioned God about something He showed me in the Bible in 1st Samuel 25 several months earlier. I knew I had heard from God about a situation that had taken place in my family at that time. Yet I would need further confirmation and revelations regarding this particular subject in order to completely understand what I was facing and how God was working in it.

Though God had started revealing to me the importance of the covenant he made through blood with Abraham via circumcision, I was not sure how that covenant would manifest in everyday life. 1st Samuel 25 never left me primarily, because it was revealed to me out of the anguish of my circumstances and earnest prayer. Also, it was the beginning of my understanding of how my theology must be consistent from Genesis to Revelation. God took me to a scripture I had no recollection of and said to me, "this is what you are dealing with," the story of Nabal, Abigal and David. Through this story God showed me why serious sickness had attacked my wife's son (my stepson). The revelation of this story was wrapped up in God's divine covering

(God's promise and protection) through a covenant man (David). Please take a moment to read the chapter for greater clarity of what I am about to share.

I had never before understood or been taught this principle of a divine covering. The scripture shows how unbeknownst to Nabal who was evil, he was being safeguarded (covered) by a righteous, covenant man. This *divine covering* sheltered everything in his household. But what hit home for me was in verse 21, which refers to being "repaid evil for good." God knew that's how I felt in my heart concerning this marriage. I was doing the best I could for my wife and her son and all I received in return was evil. I will never claim perfection or innocence but I know I was and am a covenant man. Now I know that, that alone raises a hedge or standard of protection around all that pertains to me (See Job 1). When my wife had inquired of me out of distress what was going on with her son, I feared telling her about the scripture God gave me because Nabal is described as foolish and wicked, a nature that is revealed in the interpretation of his name. What God showed me in this passage I never quite understood before, but this was an introduction to the principle of *divine covering*. When the spiritual covering is rejected or removed the enemy can move in and attack anything in the household. In this case the attack came on my stepson because God knew that it would be the only thing to capture her attention. The attack of sickness on her son would cause her to probe within herself and inquire of others, "What was going on?" This was exactly what she did.

Yet I struggled with this for quite some time because I didn't really understand how this *divine covering* worked in the context of a husband and wife. Our society has so influenced and intimidated us in our interpretation of the male and female roles in light of scripture that it is difficult to find solid ground on which to raise the standard I have been talking about throughout this book. I struggled with

the ridicule of that revelation, but never allowed myself to deny what the Lord showed me in that passage and how meaningful that discovery would be for my life eternally.

The day I sat in my living room meditating, the Lord brought this *divine covering* principle back to my mind. I really wanted to understand how I am covered, how the woman is covered, and the children are covered with super-natural promise and protection from God. What did it mean to be covered, protected or to have a divine hedge about you? How and why does God do this? As God began to pull back the curtain of concealment, I started on a journey of understanding that has forever altered my theology and I trust that it will do the same to yours. Not only that, but I trust that the world will read and accept this and be willing to allow it to be the standard for marriage, sexuality and relationships in this new millennium.

As I sat on my couch that afternoon, I began to think about my position as a New Testament believer. I realized that the blood of Jesus secures promise and protection for me. The blood is the key proponent in my salvation and also my security. Still the thing that stood out in my mind was blood and its importance to God when it comes to a covenant relationship.

As I looked back at Genesis, I saw Adam before sin with an uninterrupted relationship with God. At that point no blood was necessary because he had the promise of God's blessings and God's covering through trust and obedience. Even before the woman is brought to him he has fellowship with God based on these two components. Hence, Adam is consistently blessed by God.

I also notice that after the woman is in the garden with Adam, Gen. 2:25 says they were naked and not ashamed. This is to say they were naturally exposed yet divinely covered because of their trust and obedience. They were in perfect fellowship with one another and with God all based on trust and obedience; there they are covered by the direct presence of God. His presence or covering is unhindered because of this unobstructed relationship. They do not see their nakedness (they see themselves in a spiritually covered state); therefore there is no need for blood (or a blood covering). But notice what happens in chapter 3 as the enemy seeks first to destroy the trust of Adam and the woman. Keeping in mind that trust and obedience is the essence of their pure fellowship.

The thing Satan does in order to interrupt the established relationships is to attack the divine order, which intern brings **someone** into distrust and disobedience. This divine order is acknowledged throughout the Bible but especially highlighted in 1st Corinthians 11:3 and Ephesians 5:23 please take a moment to read these passages for clarity in this area. Satan attacks God's divine order by dealing directly with the woman outside of the context of her husband. This creates the opportunity for the woman to break relationship with her husband, who is according to 1st Corinthians 11:3, her head (responsible party). It is important to note that I do not suggest that she is incapable of functioning as an individual, however, because the husband represents the responsible party in the marriage, she should not have acted alone.

The subtlety of Satan starts with "Did God say...?" The suggestion here is, maybe you have interpreted this information incorrectly. He approaches the woman from a position of uncertainty as if to say, "Are you sure?" Normally, this tactic works best when information has passed along from another party, which constitutes hearsay. Genesis 2:16, 17 describes for us the command given to Adam, the woman was yet to be made. Therefore, I believe because there is no account of the command being given to the woman by God, Adam was the deliverer of the command to Eve as to the prohibited activity. This makes it "hearsay."

She did not have the same confidence as Adam would have, given the same circumstance. Furthermore, we notice the woman quotes the command differently than the way it is quoted in Gen. 2:16, 17, she uses the words "touch it" and "lest ye die." This further supports the fact that she likely received the command via Adam and reinterpreted it. As a result Satan quickly discredits and diffuses the most crucial part of the command. The consequences! The same way he does today. Diminish or remove the penalty and the crime will be committed. If sin has no real consequences, I might as well try it. Satan strategically negotiates with the woman not Adam. I don't believe Adam is a part of these dealings and the woman acts alone. I don't believe a <u>perfect</u> Adam would have stood for this type of strange conversation and manipulation knowing what God commanded. A sinful, weak, intimidated man may have, but we are talking about a perfect Adam who has dominion over every beast of the field (Genesis 2:19, 20). With that kind of authority and command, I don't see Adam submitting to a talking serpent that he named just days earlier. I'm thinking practically here so I'm sure you get the picture.

Adam is in a perfect relationship with God. Adam is the son of God. They commune all the time, the earth belongs to him, he talks with God in the cool of the day, and Adam is God's man! I believe Genesis 3:6, just as some other events described in Genesis chapters 1-4 take some deep yet practical thought to understand. I have to use my thoughtful, cautious, yet spiritual imagination to understand that it is quite feasible for Eve to take the fruit (after submitting to Satan) carry it, think about it, look at it some more, recognize that she did not die from touching it, go to her husband, charmed him, eat it in his presence, and then give it to Adam to eat. I further believe in this scenario because in verse 12, Adam doesn't blame the serpent, he blames the woman. If he had been present at the time of the serpent's deception why would he blame the woman? Obviously he was not present; however, the woman blames the serpent. Each one blames the one who coerced them. 1 Timothy 2:14 says, that Adam was not deceived but Eve was. This is what God has shown me to help me understand several things about this Genesis passage that has remained abstract and obscure over the years. There is no attempt here to add to the Word of God, but as in so many cases when reading the Word of God; the practical eye is often an avenue to a new revelation.

Genesis chapter 3:7 reveals the results of their sin. Relationships that were solely based on God's command and man's trust and obedience are now severed. The first aspect of this separation is spiritual. The spiritual covering that allowed them to be totally exposed and not ashamed was removed. Suddenly the protection God provided for their eyes and knowledge base was lifted and they knew that they were naked (refer to Leviticus 18 for more insight). They immediately knew what was good and what was evil. They were not privy to this before now. God knew that for them to know evil, as a fleshly being would be too much for them to handle and still maintain their spiritual relationship with him. Once evil came into the picture, the flesh would eventually have to be destroyed because it became empowered. Now the man's flesh would begin to exert its will against the man's spirit, and the eternal human struggle would begin.

Once they realized that the spiritual (divine) covering was removed, they immediately attempted to replace it with a man made or natural covering. This also suggests their immediate alienation from God spiritually. They covered themselves almost as if to deceive an all knowing God. To this day mankind still practices this method of dealing with God. We hide behind money, power, intelligence, and presentation to cover our sin, knowing that it is insufficient to recapture our relationship with God. It's even to the place now where the church promotes false coverings. By our own presentation we give many people a false sense of security, and in fact endorse hypocrisy. How many priest or preachers have told you saying a certain prayer, giving a certain amount of money, or meeting a certain quota, would put you back in right relationship with God? How often have pastors let certain persons continue in sin because of their respect for their status, money, fame or office and not dealt with their insufficient covering and unrighteous lifestyle.

Parents must begin to deal with their children by teaching and training them to acknowledge God properly so they won't create a false system of belief in their lives. The reason why this present generation is without standards is because they have not had any set for them by their parents either by example or principle. So consequently they have created their own standards and they have no merit or foundation. Pastors and church leaders must emphasize in the ears of believers everywhere the importance of a true covering in order to embrace a true relationship with God. Fostering hypocrisy has rendered the church impotent and empty. When Jesus deals with the woman at the well in Samaria (John 4), his desire is to move her away from a weak religious form, to true worship based on a spiritual relationship. We must redirect the people of the world regardless of their religious persuasion; back to true intimacy with God based on His standards not ours.

Genesis 3:7 is most revealing as to how we as human beings have spent a lifetime attempting to cover ourselves. Many are in hell today because they thought their own covering was sufficient. Maybe they thought that mother or father's covering was sufficient. Maybe they thought having their name on a church role was sufficient or holding a position in the church was sufficient or giving a large donation was sufficient. Part of the deception of the devil is to make you feel like you can satisfy God's disappointment and wrath with a manmade gift.

It seems that this act of disobedience took Adam and Eve from a God consciousness to self-consciousness. This caused them to go to great lengths to cover themselves. In the same context we can also acknowledge the conspiracy of Adam and Eve in sewing the fig leaves together. Obviously great thought, creativity and discovery went into devising a means to cover themselves. Limited resources meant working together for a solution.

It is incumbent upon pastors and believers to begin to announce again with vigor an enthusiasm; there is no human method that is sufficient to satisfy God's disappointment with us when we sin. God provided for Himself a way in Genesis just as he did in the New Testament, with a spotless lamb.

(That God was in Christ reconciling the world to Himself, not imputing their trespasses to them, and has committed to us the word of reconciliation. 2nd Corinthians 5:19)

Adam, where are you?

It is obvious that one of the undertones of this book is manly responsibility. The marines used to advertise that they were looking for a few good men. There is also a cliché that says 'a good man is hard to find'. I recently preached a message called, "Where is the man?" from John 8, using the story of the woman caught in adultery. It seems that though there are a lot of males in the world, there are few **real** men.

In the days of chivalry, the term man suggested macho, assertive, responsible, powerful and manly. Nowadays, the term man barely suggests a definitive gender. When God asks the question, "Adam, where are you?" I believe he was looking for what he had created first, and gave responsibility to, that is **the man**. Even if we consider the call to be directed to both Adam and the woman because they are one, Adam responding first says that he knew he was responsible.

Going back to Genesis, chapter 3:8 is where this sad story gets worse. First, we get a sense that possibly God's meeting Adam in the cool of the day is a ritual, especially because God asked the rhetorical question "Adam, where are you?" The voice of God is here personified, as so many things about God often are. They heard the voice walking…(KJV) they knew the voice, it was easily distinguishable, and it was the only other voice they knew, and it seems to be traveling through the garden like someone on foot. Maybe its power began rustling leaves or crunching grass or pounding the ground as it traveled. Nevertheless, it was so unnerving that Adam and his wife hid within the trees. Notice again the self-delusion of thinking they can hide from God. This was another true sign of a broken relationship. First they think they can escape the consequences of death (Satan's manipulation: "you will not surely die"), then they think they can cover themselves, and now they feel they can hide from God. Panch in Hebrew, is the word for presence, it can also mean, the face of. So they tried to hide from the all-encompassing presence of God...how absurd is that!

God's call to Adam is just that, a *call* to Adam. God calls the *responsible* party, the head of the union and says, "Where are you?" **Men** pay close attention to this question. It gives insight to how God deals with family sin throughout the Bible. How many times do we see the term the "sins of the father" (never sins of the mother) in the Bible? God is serious when it comes to the accountability of the head (See Exodus 20:5). It suggests that it will serve no purpose to redirect the rest of the body if the head is misguided. The challenge remains the same today.

Recent men's ministry movements have highlighted this fact. God's approach to the world, the church, the community, the family and even women is based on the men that have infected or affected that situation. God, have mercy on us men.

I believe the call to Adam is more a spiritual call than a geographical call. Certainly it is rhetorical. It is designed for the one being questioned to think about the question and the answer, rather than give the answer. "ADAM, where are you?" The more I write it the louder it sounds. Would you mind if I project some anger and thunder in that call? When the one who knows exactly where you are, asks where you are, it induces suspenseful concern as to what He will do when Adam finally answers or what He will do when He ultimately *finds* him. It brings to mind the times when my Mom or Dad called me, knowing where I was. The sound of their voice increased the fear. I knew I was in trouble before I revealed myself. "ADAM, WHERE ARE YOU?" Show yourself, make yourself known, come out of hiding! I know you haven't left the garden, but obviously you have left your relationship with me. Man, husband, father, stepfather, uncle, son, nephew, teacher, head, leader, lover, friend, protector, WHERE ARE YOU?

Obviously by his absence at the cool of the day something is wrong. Physically he's around but spiritually he has abandoned me. In the natural he's in the vicinity but in the spiritual he isn't recognizable. That immediate disconnection was and is a consequence of lack of trust and disobedience. Death begins in the spiritual and ends in the natural (refer to Romans 5:12). The death that Adam and Eve were probably expecting was a physical death. But the death they were experiencing was spiritual; they were cut off from freely communing with their Father and Creator. Their act of disobedience removed their *divine covering* and suddenly they became exposed to one another. This is where death starts, but it finishes in the body.

Romans 6:23 says, "The wages of sin is death," and this explains why Jesus could not stay in the grave. Jesus had never sinned, never broke the law, never disobeyed, he never distrusted his Father, and therefore death could not hold him. Death could claim his physical body because God **put our sins** on him, but it could not claim his spirit since he never violated God's laws. Therefore, Jesus had to get up from the grave. Surely Adam and Eve will die, but for now they will live reaping the consequences of their actions and become alienated from a perfect relationship with God.

Let's look closely at Adam's response. God's attention and focus is only on Adam; Adam must respond. Look at what Adam labels as his reasons for not being in his proper *spiritual and physical* position. "I heard, I was afraid, I am naked, and I hid." Upon hearing the call he should have answered but because he is out of relationship/communion it creates alienation and fear. Trust and obedience no longer cover Adam. He is frightened and scared a sign that he is out of spiritual position with God. He has never experienced anything like this before now. He is naked physically and spiritually. Because of this new knowledge he sees (naturally) with a different perspective. But he is naked spiritually because he is no longer covered by his unobstructed relationship with God. Bear in mind this relationship is purely based on trust and obedience.

Now this nakedness causes further action on the part of Adam, he hides. He tries his best to conceal or make himself secret so that his failure is not discovered, not realizing he is already *dis-covered.*

Most of us can identify with every feeling, every emotion, and every act that Adam participated in. We have all tried in some way to avoid the reality of our disconnection with God. But we have to roll the tape back here long enough to re-examine one of his answers. In particular when he says, "I'm naked." Why was Adam still saying, he was naked. Didn't he and Eve previously sew fig leaves together and cover themselves. Surely the leaves were sufficient and served the purpose intended. Yet Adam still declares, "I'm naked." Why? Well, quite frankly he was. Adam knew that his feeble attempt at reconciling his lack of trust and disobedience with fig leaves wasn't good enough.

The covering of the body had nothing to do with the covering of his spirit or his disconnection with his maker. His *spiritual covering* was based solely on an unobstructed relationship. The fig leaves represented what we all try to do at some point, a quick fix! Patch work. A band-aid on a gunshot wound (refer to Jeremiah 6:14). Good intentions, bad results. Simply put, it is nothing more than an *attempt.* But the covering must always come from the **head** of the relationship, in this case that head is God. So Adam knows that in the face of God he is still naked.

God asks Adam two questions. Notice God has not addressed the woman yet! He is dealing solely with the responsible party, the head, and the target. The two questions in verse 11 are, "who told you, you were naked?" and "have you eaten of the tree **I commanded you** not to eat of?" Adam doesn't answer the questions.

Is this not an insight as to how men typically function when confronted with failure or exposure of their guilt? We avoid the real issue and shift the blame. If men are honest they will admit to operating this way most of their lives. Why? Unquestionably it is because we are sinful individuals, who walk in the nature of Adam. But also because of how we are taught as men from childhood. Certainly, our parents have only taught us by way of their own pitfalls. But a deeper look into the psyche of a male child reveals that he does not view himself as solely accountable to his head, which is God. He often views himself as accountable to the one that has nurtured him or someone that reminds him of a nurturer. Thus, yielding to and feeling obligated to fulfill the desires of a woman. I believe men tend to give in to women because they are over-nurtured. I addressed this earlier in the chapter "Over-nurtured and Under-developed."

Adam misinterpreted the role that his wife should play in his life. Sure Adam was accountable to his wife to cover, protect and provide for her. But he is in no way obligated to respond to her in light of the command of God.

Could you imagine the pilot of a jetliner feeling more obligated to the co-pilot, when the tower has given specific instructions? The co-pilot has important information but the tower has not only a better perspective but also the last word. Maintaining the chain of command is as important as the command itself.

Adam not only passes the blame to Eve but he also distances himself from her as his suitable partner. He says to God in verse 12, "The woman you gave me, she gave me of the tree and I did eat." Almost as if to say, *it wasn't my fault God, it was her and your fault.* But Adam is at the same time denying the commandment as well as the relationship he has with God as being preeminent. How often have we men destroyed our relationships with women by blaming them for something they **offered us**, all the while knowing God has already **commanded us** to stay away from it. Gentlemen it doesn't matter if she's offering, if God says you can't have it, you can't have it! We have got to value the favor of a relationship with God (heavenly) over the compromise of a relationship with a woman (earthly).

Genesis 16:2. Look at poor confused Abram as he hearkens to the voice of Sarai. Now, I'm quick to acknowledge that one of the real problems we face today is that so many men don't hear from God and haven't heard from God in so long, that women don't trust that they will ever hear from God. This causes a godly woman to arise and take charge in the absence of a covenant man. But the problem is that this does not exempt the man or change the obligation he has of being accountable to hearing from God. That's why it is so important for a woman to only link up with a man who has a greater spiritual commitment than herself. Sidebar…a quick glance at Adam before Eve shows that he had a relationship with God, major intellectual capacity (Gen. 2:19, 20), and an occupation or purpose. (Gen. 2:15) After discerning these attributes a woman can feel more assured about a man's ability to lead her and the family.

Most women tend to connect with a man they feel they can nurture and care for, because of their nurturing make-up. But this encourages or creates dependent male characteristics, which in turn causes the man to be accountable to the woman over God. This eventually works against the relationship; especially when children come along and the woman begins to feel overwhelmed with all of her responsibilities. At that point she would prefer a leader, a decision-maker, a visionary, a protector, and a provider, someone she can lean on rather than vice versa.

God in due course addresses the woman only because there are several parties involved in this sinful act. When God asks her what is this that you have done? She answers in the same context (refer to Acts 5:9 for a similar example of this) as her husband. She gives an excuse that redirects the attention and blame. Again, if the head is misguided so goes the body. *The body functions in response to instructions that are initiated from the brain (head).* A man should never blame a woman, who he is supposed to be the head of, before he first examines himself. In most cases, the woman in his life is in some way mimicking or following the example of what she sees in the head. Therefore, she cannot be blamed without it being a mirror image of the head. Whenever you look at a woman who has gone astray it pays to reflect on the dominant male influences in her life (or absent from her life) before judgement is cast.

The term that Eve uses to describe why she did what she did is interesting. She says, "The serpent beguiled me." (not discerning who was behind the serpents ability) Beguiled, "nasha" in Hebrew, means to be "led" astray. This lends insight to where the error began. New Testament leadership is God leads Christ, Christ leads the man, and man leads the woman (1 Corinthians 11:3). When the leadership paradigm started from the bottom it led Eve astray, and then Adam, notice the error. 1st Peter 3:1 encourages the wife to be subject to her *own* husband. Which is really saying to be in submission to the man you are privately, intimately, and uniquely joined to via marriage. Because of the **secrecy** and

personalization of that relationship you can only give yourself in submission to him, and **absolutely no one else**. In light of this Eve should not have been led or submitted to anyone else.

It's important to note that these divinely inspired verses aren't designed to suppress or hinder a woman but rather to protect and cover her. This also releases her from the fear of being manipulated or abandoned after having submitted herself lovingly to a man. The resentment and resistance we experience today is only a result of men not understanding their role and women submitting to the wrong men for the wrong reasons. In fact, submission for every woman should start with her father. As she relates to and identifies with his love, protection and authority in the home growing up it becomes easier to parallel that to her husband. Ideally, this would constitute a relationship of unconditional love without manipulation for personal gain.

Men don't realize they are the targets of the devil when it comes to the family. The man is the responsible party. Unfortunately men have misinterpreted this positioning by God and made it a position of dictation, exploitation and manipulation. The fact of the matter is when men abuse their position as head their head chastises them, which is Christ.

To further encourage the power and grace of a woman concerning her husband, 1st Peter 3:5 talks about how awesome a position she holds when she walks adorned with holiness and trust. This is the greatest influence you can have on a man in allowing him to acknowledge his position of being subject to Christ. Peter uses the example of Sarah to encourage women to be like her daughters. He tells them not to be fearful of manipulation and do what is right in the sight of God and God will bless you as Sarah was blessed, even though she was tested (refer to Genesis 13:2, 17:15, 16; 21:1-3).

The important thing, especially for the women of the

next generation, is not to link themselves with men that do not walk in a covenant relationship with God. This will minimize the fear of being manipulated. A woman must allow God to bring the man into her life who is able to recognize who she is. Proper identification as in Genesis 2:22, 23 is the key. Adam knew who the woman was and where she came from. The real test of whether or not you are uniting with the right man is in his spiritual ability to identify you. *Obviously, you must know yourself first.* So often relationships between men and women have gone awry simply because the man did not discern why God brought that person into his life.

Now the reason why the onus is on the man is because regardless of what a woman may present to him he must know how to redirect her based on his covenant relationship with God and the standards God has imputed upon him. This covenant relationship allows him to look at a woman and not automatically think romance or that which is simply self-gratifying, even if she is offering romance. This is the one insight I wish I had growing up. If I had been taught or indoctrinated this way, beauty, aspiration and lust would not have had such a heavy influence on me. Instead, I would have discerned with each woman I met that first and foremost my covenant relationship overrode my carnal way of looking at them. My priority would have been to love, protect and determine who she was first, without the attachment of romance. This factor becomes so paramount when men are dealing with women outside of romance, even if there is an attraction.

Let us go back to Genesis 3:13. God spends no time in dialogue with Eve. He accepts her answer and moves on to the serpent. Why? It's because God does not look at her as the standard bearer. Adam was the standard bearer in this union. Since she said she was led astray by the serpent God moves on to the serpent. Notice that no questions are asked of the serpent. Why? There is no need, we all know serpents don't talk! The serpent was the instrument of the devil, used for that moment. But as a tool of the enemy it would receive a curse that would remind mankind forever of the incident in the garden. God curses the serpent above every other beast by restricting it to crawl in the dust of the earth. This is an interesting <u>curse</u> for the serpent, being that man came from the dust of the earth. Somehow I believe there is a connection. It may simply be that the serpent will never rise above man ever again.

The curse continues with the noted hatred and hostility that will be between the woman and the serpent. Then God's focus shifts to the future. For that which comes from the woman (the Son of God) will be bruised at the heel by what comes from the enemy. But her offspring will crush or destroy the offspring of the enemy. This deals with Christ ability to walk the earth and conquer sin and the anti-Christ at the end.

It is comforting to note that in the context of Christ the Son of God, God would not have to endure the same disappointment as with Adam. Jesus would be found willing and worthy to present himself before God when called to take the blame for all of mankind. When Adam would shift the blame, Jesus would take the blame. Even in the Garden of Gethsemane, when Jesus would have preferred to take a different route, he is **found** of his Father when called to take the place and accept the penalty for sins he **did not** commit.

So where are the men? I know that most of them are in hiding or disguised, but my prayer is that they will come out of hiding, take off the mask, stop the charade and be counted worthy of the designation we have been given by God. **Man.**

Truth and Consequences

Genesis chapter 3 reveals truth and consequences. We can learn so much about who we are and what God intends for us by just accepting the truth about the consequences described in this chapter. Both men and women have tried to dodge the ultimatums of God, but as long as we live and breathe what God has spoken he has spoken. There is not a human being alive that can change what God has proclaimed. Continue the journey with me through chapter 3 of Genesis.

When we left off from this chronology of events we were dealing with the curse placed upon the serpent for its participation in the downfall of man. Next, God shifts to the woman, not with curses but with truth and consequences. The consequence has 4 forms of manifestation, (1) sorrows, (2) difficulty or pain in pregnancy, (3) a longing or desire for her husband, and (4) he will rule over you. Understanding these four aspects of the consequence gives great insight to womanhood. Most men are never taught to understand or deal with the deep internal aspects of womanhood. Therefore, most men become guilty of some form of abuse of women. Extreme sensitivity is necessary in dealing with women because of their make up.

The first aspect of the consequence highlights "sorrows" interpreted pain, difficulty, and emotions. They

are greatly increased in her. The scripture says, "In multiply-
ing, I will multiply." Whereas the man did not receive these
consequences, there is an obvious difference between men
and women. I've heard some women say; "I wish I weren't
so emotional," and now I understand why they say it. It's
truly a consequence of Eve's sin. But I believe we have the
liberty to look for the good in every situation. So, this
increase of emotional response is a very necessary balance in
the male and female relationship. But if it is not understood
and accepted, then it will be problematic and despised.

It is so important for a woman to use her emotions
for sensitivity in her relationship. Some decisions warrant
emotional input, though they should not always be made
emotionally. It brings a healthy balance to the temperament
of the home. More importantly, children need a healthy
emotional deposit as a part of their nurturing process. Our
spiritual experience is sometimes authenticated by emotion-
alism. We relate to the world emotionally in order to sense
commonality. Yet the biggest difficulty is when men reject
women's emotions and mistake them for weakness or frailty.
This is why so many women gravitate to other women. It is
also why the potential for lesbianism exists. The common
ground of emotional compatibility is sometimes confused
and made to be something romantic. In fact, it is just the
common ground found with someone of a similar makeup.

Part two of the consequence deals with the toil of
pregnancy and the difficulty associated with bringing children
into the world. As advanced as we are, the reality remains that
the nine months of pregnancy and the delivery of a child are
still difficult. The truth is it will never change. Doctors may
use drugs and technology but without these tools there is no
doubt that childbirth is painful. But this sensitivity to pain
doesn't have to be despised. It can serve as a tool in relating
to God and sensing the burden of prayer. This is especially
recognized when it comes to birthing things from the invisi-

ble to the visible. The wonderful thing is that there are thousands of times in the Bible where God acknowledges the emotional cries/prayers of his children. So we thank God that when a man may not shed a tear...a woman will!

Part three of the consequence deals with the woman's desire. God says to the woman, you will long to be with your husband intimately, romantically, and emotionally. This is so true. How many marriages have fallen apart because the woman simply longed for her husband's attention and could not get it? Longed for time to spent with him and he just couldn't understand why? Even after the pain and difficulty previously mentioned, the *wanting* for your husband will remain. Through the generations I believe that woman have tried to evolve away from this fact. More women than ever have vocalized their lack of a need for a man. But I believe this is primarily a result of the pain of disappointment, abuse and afflictions men have imputed upon women. The truth is, most women want a man! Every woman I talked with during the writing of this book, stated when it comes down to it, they would rather not be alone. But my survey has also led me to believe that they are not willing to settle as much as in the past. They don't want to be hurt again, so fear guides them towards loneliness. So if they are doing well now, they don't want that peace to be interrupted. They have raised their standards. They want someone who can make life better. Women want men in their lives and they want romance but they don't want mess.

I believe the longing is there. But in particular once the marriage vows are exchanged she becomes comfortable with giving herself to him and desires that interaction continuously. She wants the holding, the communication (verbal and non-verbal), the lovemaking, the planning, the goal setting, and the life of love.

Lastly, God adds to the consequence something that is exacted upon her. Everything else is a part of her. But now

God says, "And he shall rule over you" (referring to the husband). The same Hebrew word is used in Genesis 1:18 and 4:7, it means to govern or dominate, have power or reign over. In my lifetime this has always been looked at in a negative way. Coming of age in a woman's liberated society I have not known many American women in particular, to rest easy with this part of the consequence. But let us examine it and grasp its deepest principle.

First, the expression "he shall rule over you" doesn't refer to every man! Just the one you are in covenant relationship with. So there is the **security** of marriage. Keep in mind you will only link in marriage to one you are compatible with. This governing is not for public display of power, but rather it is to maintain the standard for your home, which has been commanded of God through your husband, who had a relationship with God before the wife came along (see Gen. 2:15-20). This in fact makes good sense, because every earthly relationship has these boundaries. Look at your relationship with government, your job, your school, your parents, the motor vehicle department, etc. We are governed in every relationship so as to eliminate chaos. But more importantly we must acknowledge the *uniqueness* of these relationships. For example, with a driver's license every one who has one is governed by the basic rules of the road. However, depending on the class of license one person can drive an eighteen-wheeler, and another can not drive without supervision. The rules are designed to keep everyone on the road safe. If the rules are ignored, accidents happen.

That's why to be *governed* by your covenant husband is a good thing! It eliminates chaos while at the same time highlights the *uniqueness* of that relationship. You see, once the man gives to his wife the standard that God has given him for his home, that standard *governs* both of them and *protects* both of them.

Once Eve allowed herself to be governed by the

words of the serpent, with which she had no covenant, she was led astray and broke the intimate fellowship she had with her husband. She was governed by the wrong influence. We are all ruled in one aspect or another. But when it comes to marriage, God has set up these boundaries primarily to keep us from duplicating the mishap of Adam and Eve. This also creates the most private and intimate kind of relationship imaginable.

Next, Genesis 3:17-19 is devoted to the consequences Adam receives from God. The first part of the statement is most indicting. When it comes to leadership or responsibility you must remember to whom you are obligated. God goes straight to the root of the problem. Because you hearkened to (shama in Hebrew), gave attention to, consented to, were obedient to the *loud call* (qol / qowl in Hebrew) of your wife, you are reaping this consequence. It's interesting that the next time this word shama is used in the Bible it is talking about Abram doing the same thing with his wife Sarai. The issue wasn't whom he listened to as much as whose voice he forsook. King Saul in 1 Samuel 15:24 realized that for listening to the people and not God, it cost him his kingship. God wanted Adam to honor their relationship above every other relationship; this is what got Adam in trouble! Men will always be given options about the standards they have, but he is only to consider them in the context of what God has commanded first.

With Adam, God says *why* he is receiving the consequence, with Eve and the serpent there is no explanation. This gives further insight into how God saw the sin and the standard bearer. For all of those who believe God commanded Eve it is obvious here that Adam commanded Eve, not God. Therefore when he deals with Adam he is highlighting (even in this rebuke) the relationship they had. It's almost as if God is saying, "How could you, Adam? I commanded you...my relationship with you was first!" This was to remind Adam of what they shared before Eve came along. God then tells him the consequence of his actions.

He starts with cursing the ground because of him. The Hebrew term "arar" is used which is interpreted, execrate. This means, to express detestation for or to abhor. So because Adam came from the earth, God is cursing the earth. This helps us understand why God was sorry that he ever made man when he destroyed the earth by flood. It was almost a building up of "arar." Previously the earth was a blessing to Adam and it served him. But now the earth would become a detestable place that he would have to struggle in and survive in.

The truth is that throughout history we have seen how the earth has revolted against man. The power of nature is uncontainable. Volcanoes, earthquakes, tidal waves, hurricanes, famines, pestilence and natural disasters are out of the control of man. One day it's beautiful and the next it's taking your hope away. In the morning the storm can rage unrelenting, while in the evening you can look up and see the stars. So, the earth can be our haven and our horror.

Adam is relegated to consuming or feeding off of the earth for all of his days. The only difference now is that it will be in sorrow. The same term used by God in the case of the woman. But here it's not multiplied. God says that through painful toiling, you will work the earth and eat of it. Notice the woman does not reap this consequence, only the man. This is one of those areas that have created such difficulty for men and women.

Quite simply it is outlined here how the head would be responsible for the supplying of the physical needs of himself, his wife, and his family. How many couples would have survived if they were not both working the ground? How many women would not have married if they had known and understood the purpose of this context? The man should be capable of presenting to the woman his potential for providing for her physical well being **completely**. At the same time, this will not be easy for the man. His toiling takes affect on him. Sometimes it becomes frustrating but not to the degree that his *emotions* will be the driving force behind his behavior. Yet this will be the case as long as he is alive. However, the original interpretation also suggests 'as long as he has strength or appetite'.

What we have seen over the years with some men who have abandoned their responsibilities is that they have no strength or no appetite anymore. There is no passion to work the earth. So women have refused to starve, they have evolved to the position of providing for themselves. This has changed the positioning of men in two ways. They have lost their appetite and defaulted to hearkening to the voice of the women in their life and not the voice of God. Why, because the woman being the provider, creates psychological and material leverage in their relationship. Keep in mind God's design has nothing to do with how we view one another and everything to do with His divine order. God's order is not designed for one party to feel superior to the other but rather to distinguish our roles and eliminate the subliminal competition and/or equality struggle that so often distracts men and women from the joy of being who they are, together. Men have to get back to understanding how important it is to work the ground and relieve the women of this task especially because working the ground is not her consequence.

Next, God says to Adam, that the same earth you must work will produce difficulty for you. Verse 18 refers to "thorns and thistles" and the herb of the field. Putting these together shows how man will eat of the earth but it will be difficult retrieving the fruit or the prosperity thereof. The earth will produce prosperity and benefit for him to provide for his family, but while it does that it won't be easy to achieve those results. The truth is that men have been trying forever to get around this fact. Easy money and get rich quick schemes are often the downfall of many. God will allow you to be blessed but it won't be easy. Remember this is a consequence of disobedience. This is a part of the suffering brought on by sin.

God follows it up in verse 19 with an emphasis on "the sweat of thy face, you will eat bread." Highlighting again that physical exertion that causes perspiration and weakens the body will be the means by which you will survive. Once again, I emphasize that this is exclusive to the man and not the woman. Why? Obviously, because suffering and sweat and struggle of bringing children into the world was enough! The man's consequence is hard work in order to eat! The woman has emotional strain and pregnancy pain, needs and desires that will plague her, but not the working of the ground in order to provide for the family. This is one of the greatest areas of difficulty in our society today. The inability for the woman to trust and rely on the man to provide for her without manipulation and exploitation is almost insurmountable. Instead in most marriages both man and woman are working and instead of *complimenting* one another they end up *competing* against one another. God clearly puts these consequences upon the man because of his disobedience towards him. Prior to his sin, the earth was designed to serve Adam, now Adam would have to work the earth. Furthermore, it would serve as a constant reminder as to where he was headed when he died. God says to him, from the ground you were taken! Now you will work it, struggle with it, fight it, and ultimately return to it. So now the realization is that God is confirming what he said initially… "In the day you eat of it, you shall surely die." Now Adam knows his destination is death. After all of the blood, sweat and tears, he is doomed to return to dust. Hebrews 9:27 says, "It is appointed to man once to die and after that the judgement." So after Adam's departure he would be examined and judged for everything that he did while he was on the earth.

After digesting all of the repercussions for sin I notice Adam's functions in the same capacity intellectually as before. This is a blessing and an important note. Verse 20 states, Adam called his wife "Eve", Charrah in Hebrew, which is interpreted "life giver" or spring of life. Most times we feel God demotes us, takes away our ability or capability based on our distrust and disobedience. That is not always true. In particular here Adam still functions as he has been made to function. He recognizes who his wife is in purpose and destiny. So he appropriately names her Eve. One of the things I think women should be aware of is *"Does the man I plan to marry or am presently involved with, know who I am"?* Has God given him the capacity to properly identify me? If he doesn't, he will more than likely misuse and abuse you. If he doesn't know who you are, he's not one!

Now we get to the most meaningful part of the passage. This is where God's anger and disappointment is finally released and resolved. Verse 21 says God made coats of skin for Adam and his wife and clothed them. Several things are established here in this one verse. Let's look at them.

First there seems to be a sense of oneness in the language, "Adam and his wife," not Adam and Eve, which would denote individuality. Married couples must constantly remind themselves that spiritually they are one flesh. Couples must embrace this oneness, two persons but one entity in the eyes of God. The term Adam and his wife really refers to, Adam and she who is a part of him. Even in the midst of failure, couples have to maintain the reality of oneness.

Next, "God makes..." or creates something *new*, conceptually, the creation of clothing not from leaves but from skin. Obviously, the covering of fig leaves was insufficient. Adam knew it that's why he hid when he heard God walking in the cool of the day. The leaves represented a man made covering but did not satisfy God's requirement for remission of sins. It may have partially covered the body from an external perspective, but sin goes much deeper than the external. Sin produced spiritual nakedness, spiritual shame, and spiritual separation. Sin broke Adam's relationship with his father, sin diminished Adam's dominion over the earth, and sin severed the purity of Adam's relationship with his wife.

Certainly fig leaves could not rectify these areas of nakedness and shame. Man has followed Adam's example for years and has been hiding ever since. We know our way falls short and is terribly insufficient but we still hide behind our man-made covering. Fig leaves of pride, money, titles and status are all insufficient coverings for sin. Only blood quells the rage and wrath of the God who demands obedience.

In light of that, God in his all-surpassing and infinite wisdom slays an animal to retrieve its skin and use it for a bloody covering for Adam and his wife. The Bible doesn't say what animal skin was used but I believe and understand that an animal must have been slain in order for its skin to be used.

I would like to believe it was a lamb. I use this parallel because God refers to his son Jesus as "the Lamb of God (see John 1:29) that takes away the sins of the world." Isn't it interesting that God calls his son a *lamb* and at the same time one of our primary forms of fabric is wool! So to this day we often cover ourselves with the coat of the animal God most likely used to cover Adam and Eve.

Now for the first time Adam and Eve understand what it means to God when they sin and what has to be done to satisfy his wrath. His anger must have been displayed right before their eyes. Imagine if you would the horror of the moment.

God commands Adam and Eve to sit on a rock while

he begins the process of subduing his wrath. They have no idea what He is about to do. Suddenly the hand of God snatches an animal with a sufficient outer coat of skin. He violently slams it to the ground. It's bruised and disoriented. Then he flips it over on its back and cuts it down the middle. Blood spurts everywhere, a sickening shriek erupts from the traumatized animal. God forcefully splits it in two and it jerks a few last times before its innocent life is emptied out. Adam and Eve experience the introduction to death at the hands of God.

Now God begins to peal away the skin from the body, neatly, meticulously, and painstakingly. There is blood on the ground. Suddenly, it hits Adam; innocent blood has to be spilled for his transgressions. One of those innocent animals only days ago he had named and played with, is now dead for his sake. A new standard is set for Adam and his wife. Whenever we distrust and disobey God, he is provoked beyond comprehension, so we must kill something innocent, something perfect, and something that has no blemishes, in order to satisfy the wrath of God. In fact Adam knew that that animal should have been him! He also knew that it could not be him, because he no longer represented innocence or obedience. God was merciful.

Next, God makes coverings out of the skin for Adam and his wife. He gives them to Adam and his wife, and when they put it on there are traces of blood on them. Now they are properly covered. They would have never known redemption without God's intervention. They are eternally grateful, for God made His own way to save them from the promised death for their actions.

From this one verse we understand that a standard of blood is instituted. Now Adam knows every covering and consequently every covenant must be ratified with blood.

From this, the story of Cain and Abel makes more sense. Surely the standard imputed upon Adam was practiced as a family standard. Therefore his children knew at the time of sacrifice for atonement for disobedience, there must be blood. Remember that Cain brought fruit for sacrifice in which there was no blood, Abel brought of his flock, an animal containing blood. "The process of time" in Genesis 4:3 suggests they were now at the age of accountability. In other words, they knew what the standard was, so it was up to them now to present offering and sacrifice to God for themselves. They knew right from wrong, acceptable from unacceptable. Therefore, Cain's sacrifice was rejected not because it wasn't the best that he had, but rather it was because it contained no blood.

Let's return to the truth and consequences of Adam and Eve. They are driven from their possession, the Garden of Eden, never to return again. But notice it is because of God's grace that they remain covered. The truth is that though their location will change, their relationship is back in tact. We know this by the blessing of long life and many offspring (refer to Genesis 5:1-5, Adam lives a long life and has many children).

From this third chapter there is a foundation set from which all of our understanding of relationships, marriage, sexuality and sex, covering and covenants are established. This information is fascinating and should be shared with every young person, single person, virgin, single parent, divorcee, homosexual, preacher, and church, everywhere.

My hope and prayer is that from this platform the insights shared here will make good sense and bring the areas of relationships we have been so confused about and confined by into perspective.

The Covering of the Covenant

Though I believe the essentials of the covenant were established in Genesis 3, we do not see the labeling of such until Noah comes on the scene in Genesis 6:18 and again throughout the ninth chapter. However, there was a distinction between the covenant with Noah and the covenant with Abram as described in Genesis chapter 15.

As I introduce the covering of the covenant, I am referring to God's promise to an individual and God's protection of that individual. Within this concept I will talk about the marriage covenant. When I talk about the covering of the covenant as it pertains to the husband and wife, I am referring to the man as the responsible party for the wife and the entire family. This responsibility includes protecting and providing for needs of the wife and family, as well as setting the standards the family will live by. When a man covers a woman, he is to be responsible for her. The kids today would say, "I got your back."

Abram asked the question of God, "How will I know that I will inherit this land?" In Genesis 15:9 God answers Abram by telling him to take certain animals and cut them in half (all but the birds). As God initiates His promise with Abram we see blood being shed in connection with this covenant. This also matches with the Hebrew word often used for covenant, which is beriyth. This word means cutting, compact, confederate, covenant or league. This begins a pattern that will be consistent throughout God's word. Covenants will always include the shedding of blood. This time Abram splits the animals in half, but the next time God speaks of a covenant to Abram he will require a different approach. The significance of bloodshed will help us understand its connection when it comes to the covenant of marriage and the initial act of sex. I'll explain this further later on in this chapter.

Take a moment to read Genesis 15, 16, 17, so that you will have knowledge of what I am going to explain throughout the balance of this chapter.

In Genesis chapter 16 Abram *hearkens* to the voice of his wife, though God had already spoken to him. This represents failure of astounding proportion. Why is this such a tragic misfortune? First, God had already spoken to Abram specifically concerning Sarai and their future. Second, Abram did exactly what Adam did by accepting *the woman's offer*. Third, Abram's seed was designated with promise and therefore was not to be deposited in anyone other than the one that God had specified as a partaker of that promise.

Abram's seed carried the power of promise and destiny and would have caused irreversible repercussions if used outside of God's expressed desire and direction. Thus the seed given to Hagar, Sarai's servant, creates this problem. The proof of the power of his seed is obvious in chapter 16:7-13, where God speaks to Hagar via the angel of the Lord and shares with her a promise *similar* to what was shared with Abram. The difference seems to be in the conduct of these descendants. Wild and rebellious will they be almost in accordance with the act of Abram rebelling against God's promise and submitting to his wife.

This highlights how important it is for the man to recognize he is the carrier of the seed of promise and destiny.

Therefore, he must discern and recognize the woman suitable to that promise in order to bring forth the offspring that represents the legacy and destiny of that union. Also, this magnifies the significance of monogamy and abstinence until marriage. If the man is ignorant of God's promise on his life and mutually doesn't discern the woman to bring forth that promise, it will create big problems.

Men have inappropriately scattered their seed and in many cases created a wild and rebellious generation of children which we have recently labeled "X." They are mostly unruly, immoral, without loyalty, rebellious, wild and misunderstood. This is a result of men planting their seed in strange and foreign vessels. Consequently, generation X'ers have a connection to a father but also a disconnection (based on covenant) that creates confusion and uncertainty within their nature. Their concept of family is distorted, their references about life are unconventional, and they have no sense of destiny passed down from their fathers because he is absent from their everyday life.

We have begun to except them in the main stream as the "hip-hop" generation, but in fact they are a generation of children that have no **fathers** to introduce them to their covenant promise. Think of the many children in our society that are only acknowledged on a part-time basis by their fathers. This would automatically mean that they are only accountable for part of the time also. This tragic reality will persist until men discern the power of promise on their lives. Men must cease to manipulate or be manipulated into sexual intercourse with a woman who is not the promised vessel for him.

One would think that God would forsake His covenant with Abram because of this act. But in fact, he re-establishes it with greater intensity. In Genesis 17, God deals with Abram again 13 years after the birth of Ishmael, Hagar's son. This indicates how much time was wasted because of Abram's failure, but also shows God's mercy in allowing Abram to focus on his son until his age of accountability (13 years old). At that point God does a couple of different things.

First, he says to Abram, walk before me and be blameless. This is God's personal challenge to him to walk holy and upright almost as a reminder of the previous failure. Second, God changes Abram's name. Names are important to God. The changing of a name often indicates a change in the nature of that person or a change of destiny. God says to him, "your name is Abraham" or 'the father of many', as opposed to Abram, which means 'high father'. This will have an effect on how he sees himself, which will affect how he lives. Third, he reiterates the promise of descendants and the land where his is a stranger will be his. Then in verse 9, the stern voice of God states, "You will keep my covenant, you and your descendants forever." (The offspring is included in the covenant or the standard)

Next, God is about to institute something that will never change. In Gen. 17:10-14, God outlines the tenant of this covenant. For the first time man will be indelibly connected to the covenant because he himself will shed the blood that ratifies it. God describes to Abraham what will happen, how it will happen and when it will happen.

God introduces circumcision, something that will be painful, something that will mark the man forever; something that will pierce the flesh and cause bloodshed, which will now be sufficient for God to recognize his covenant forever with Abraham and for Abraham to reminded of this covenant relationship. Not only that, Abraham must initiate the act with every male that is within his household whether son or servant. God also verifies that any man that is not circumcised has no covenant with him.

According to Genesis 17:12, the man must be circumcised eight days after birth, thus placing him in the covenant. Circumcision is the putting away or ripping away of the foreskin at the tip of the man's penis. Obviously this means that the sign of the covenant can only be marked on the man. This became a dilemma for me the night God spoke to me initially concerning this revelation because I knew that a woman could not be circumcised. She can only know whether or not a man has been circumcised. (This is her way of discerning a covenant man) This is when God began to clear up the assumptions and confusion that existed in my mind my entire life. No one had ever dealt with this in all of my years of being in church. No one had ever explained to me the real difference between the ways God deals with a man versus a woman. No one in my day and age had been able to properly apply the word of God to the battle of women's liberation and what God says about the headship, leadership, and responsibility of the man. So for me this was the first time it was coming together.

Remember earlier when God began to speak to me that Sunday afternoon He started with the definition of being *covered*. Covered spiritually as it relates to God's covenant, but also being covered naturally as it relates to the man and woman. The circumcision of a man is the key to the covenant. So that the covenant man covers the woman, but this is not where it ends, this is where it begins. We know that the woman of promise needs to be equally bound to the covenant with a similar form of bloodshed. So the question for me was, how?

Some might relate that bloodshed to her monthly menstrual cycle. But that can't be accurate because it is reoccurring and represents internal cleansing. Remember with Abraham the bloodshed from circumcision was painful, it was an obvious physical marking, and it happened one time. Those three characteristics are essential. So God focused my attention on something specific that would mimic the experience of the man. God in his infinite wisdom created the woman with an internal membrane tissue that partially closes her vaginal orifice. This sheath remains in tact (under normal circumstances) until the woman experiences her first act of sexual intercourse. In that first experience, the membrane (hymen) is broken or ripped, and as with the man when he is circumcised, it is painful and blood is shed. With this one time occurrence the circumcised man extends the covenant he has with God to his wife, thus making them *one flesh* in the eyes of God. This "one flesh" is a result of the connection the woman has via bloodshed (marriage covenant) to the man. The man is connected to the promise via bloodshed (circumcision covenant) to God. This acknowledges the spiritual covering that a woman must have via a covenant man.

Obviously, this highlights why it is so important for a virgin to wait until marriage for sex because the hymen can only be broken once! Therefore, if it is broken with a man that's not your husband that sexual act represents a false covenant. This transaction is not just a physical act; it is spiritual as well.

This explains why women so often can't forget their first sexual experience and why they feel attached to the man behind that experience. A false covenant means there is no remission of sin and no promise attached. Also remember, one of Eve's consequences was a desire for her husband, which means the act of sexual intercourse creates an appetite for continual sexual interaction. This physical hunger will cause a woman to be open and vulnerable over and over again to a man even though the reality is her spirit is longing for a covering, a covenant of promise and a permanent relationship.

The man's covenant marking takes place shortly after birth, however no such action can take place with the woman concerning her physical attachment to that covenant until she has sexual intercourse. In light of this, her covenant father (or a covenant man) is responsible for the woman until such time as she is given over to the covering of her covenant husband. This transaction is paramount. At this point she is joined to her covenant husband physically and covered spiritually. This is why it is so important to remain a virgin until marriage. In the man's case the power of promise in his seed will be wrongly deposited and for the woman she will forfeit her only time of sacred bloodshed without a covenant and will be open to other false covenants as she searches for the lasting one.

The tradition of a father giving away his daughter in the marriage ceremony is representative of the father giving up his responsibility to the man she will be in a new covenant relationship with. *Fathers give away daughters, not sons!*

With a clear understanding of this divinely ordained principle, abstinence becomes the only sensible approach to sexuality until marriage. Even in Genesis 17, God emphasizes that Abraham will have a child with his wife, *the vessel of promise.* I believe God is saying, "Hagar is not your wife and Ishmael is not my child of promise." In light of this God must now remind him that Sarai is the one He will acknowledge and the changing of her name to Sarah is the expression of that promise. (This is also a sign of their compatibility)

So Abraham circumcised all of the men in his household including Ishmael. All of these men were now *irreversibly* marked as covenant men. So now both man and woman are covered in God's divine plan through a *onetime* bloodshed event that ties the woman to the man and the man to God.

Note: God often uses an external insignia as a reminder of an internal commitment. The sign of the rainbow for Noah was God's external sign of an internal promise never to destroy mankind again by a flood. In the New Testament, God uses baptism as an external act for us to mark an internal change in our commitment toward a Christ-like lifestyle. In the same way circumcision was designed to be an external marking that would serve as a reminder of an internal covenant relationship between God and the man. This same dynamic is applied in the relationship between the man and his wife. Each time they enjoy sexual intimacy it is an external reminder of an internal commitment.

The difficulty for us when it comes to the external is that sometimes we allow it to have greater value or significance than the internal. I recall with great frequency as an evangelist asking people if they were saved and they would response, "I was baptized as a child in so-in-so church." For them the external had greater value than the internal. The external is only a place or time or a marking that we can use as a reference or a reminder of something that supercedes it. In the case of Abraham, God wanted him to have a permanent reminder of the promise and commitment he had established between them.

Obviously there are many men today who were not circumcised at birth and they may view this as a problem concerning the covenant. However, in Acts 15 the argument concerning the Gentiles inclusion in this Hebraic faith includes the issue of circumcision. As a result of the apostle's deliberations with the help of the Holy Spirit, they concluded that circumcision is not necessary when the man has accepted Christ as savior by faith. In fact, repentance (whether Jew or Gentile) from past sins and acceptance of Christ now represents the *circumcision of the heart* which embodies the natural circumcision of the flesh thus bringing every man who is saved into the same covenant relationship as Abraham and his household.

In addition, I return to the act of baptism as a beneficial external sign that an uncircumcised man may use for his marking. Because he is not obligated to return to the Old

Testament standard of physical circumcision, he can use this New Testament standard to highlight an internal commitment. Since the opportunity for baptism (as a sign of his covenant relationship with Christ) is more feasible than circumcision, it should be used for that purpose. Similarly a woman who has lost her virginity prior to marriage should follow this same pattern. However, it is only a reminder and doesn't exceed the value of repentance, which represents the circumcision of heart.

Fatherless

This divine design of being covered is consistent throughout the word of God. Old and New Testament support it.

To further demonstrate this principle, God never uses the term motherless in the Bible. But the term fatherless is used repeatedly. This is consistent with the covering and responsibility previously described. The covering comes from the father not the mother. Though in today's world the mother is looked upon as the most needed and necessary, spiritually it is not true. This is what the devil has capitalized on. He has convinced us all through the calamity of men, that they are not needed. Women have said, I can manage on my own, I can do badly all by myself, whatever the reasoning the man is disconnected from the home experience. Our government exacerbated it with the welfare system. In order to get assistance the man had to be absent. This has set households up to be conquered by the devil. He simply sees a headless home and it reminds him of Eve without Adam back in the garden. He knows it's vulnerable.

The woman in turn, has had to manage and evolve into something *other* than what God created in her, to maintain this dynamic called "a single parent household." This trick of the enemy has destroyed children, communities and the woman. And most of all God throughout his word acknowledges the fatherless and widows or women without husbands, as needing protection, a covering and most of all, a covenant man in their lives.

In 1 Corinthians 11:3 the prescription for the divine, sequential, arrangement of God and man is ordained to maintain order and structure. This authoritative direction is given by God to eliminate earthly debate that arises out of trend, opinion, rebellion or an absence of truth. Jesus never puts his will above that of the Father, though he describes himself as being one with the Father in John 17. This applies greatly with the married couple, though they are one, God's divine order is acknowledged in that relationship in the same way that Jesus describes him and the Father are one, yet He submits to the Father. Christ and the church represent a marriage; we are one with him, yet we submit to him as the head. The husband and wife are one, yet the woman submits to the husband as the head or the responsible party. Uniquely, the man submits to Christ as his head.

Fathers are primarily referred to throughout the Bible starting with Genesis. Just as we acknowledge the family unit today by the name of the father. But more importantly the term fatherless is found at least 43 times in the King James Version (KJV). The term widow is referred to at least 85 times in the KJV. The term motherless is not mentioned once. Once again this demonstrates the truth of God's word concerning divine covering and covenant. The preoccupation of God with widows and the fatherless children relates directly to the covenant covering of the man. In other words, who is responsible for them?

The absence of such a covering is still of major concern to God. In Exodus 22:22-24, God sets forth his standard concerning the treatment of those who have lost their husbands or fathers. Simply put, "If you hurt or take advantage of them, I will destroy you." The Hebrew word used in the Old Testament is yathowm, which means to be lonely, bereaved, or *fatherless* referring to children or an orphan. The gentleness of God comes through here and it is obvious that this covering is a great necessity.

Deuteronomy 10:18 demonstrates how God will deal justly with the fatherless and with widows by feeding and clothing them. Deut. 14:29 explains how men must share goods from their own inheritance with the widow, stranger, and fatherless due to their lack of inheritance and provision. The inheritance referred to here is the legacy of the covenant man. This in turn infers that the inheritance of the widow and her children is directly related to what the father leaves for them. The absence of a father or a covenant man automatically suggests there will be no inheritance. Many will believe that this was a result of the times in which they were living and women were uneducated and couldn't provide for themselves. This was true, however in many cases this still holds true today. Maybe this statement does not hold true as much in developed countries, but it still exist in a large portion of the modern world. The reason is because God's truth will never change.

The consequences of Eve's action in the garden was not "working the ground to eat" and to provide for her household, that was Adam's consequence. God's standard remains the same. Deut. 24:17-22 once again highlights the compassion that must be exhibited to the stranger, the fatherless and the widow. It is mentioned almost as if it is a remembrance to the days of being a stranger in Egypt and being a slave. God says when you harvest the land what ever is missed the first time, don't go back and get it. Rather leave it for those who are without a covering, a provider, or a protector (refer to Deut. 26:12, 13 and 27:9).

Esther 2:7 says that Esther had neither father nor mother, so Mordecai her uncle took her as his own daughter. This was a sign of his covenant relationship with God, and his proper discerning of his relationship with his niece. If only we had more uncles who would honor their covenant with God by taking care of their nieces and nephews as their own children, as opposed to abusing and manipulating them. Thank God for Mordecai, he knew who he was and he knew the purpose he should play in Esther's life. When a man *knows his purpose*, he will not *abuse* what God puts under his authority.

In Ruth chapter 2, the young widow Ruth was allowed to go into the field to glean grain after the reapers were finished. Her covenant man died before they could have children and there was no inheritance for her. As a result of this she was an uncovered woman. However, she found favor in the eyes of Boaz the owner of the field, and he began to cover (be responsible for) her life. These two instances show continuity with the verses in Deuteronomy.

This gives clear insight to God's expectation with regards to the covering of a widow or orphans. Moreover God's anger is displayed in Isaiah 10:1, 2 as he issues a "woe" to those leaders who set themselves against widows, fatherless and the poor. Evidently manipulation of the powerless is what angers God. Today many women refuse to acknowledge powerlessness, yet I have never heard of a man being raped by a woman. Powerlessness can be manifested in several different ways. Our society continually empowers women, but the observations made throughout the Bible show that God's perspective remains the same. The problem we face today is primarily due to men that have stepped out of place; they no longer cover and protect women. Therefore, women have been forced to adapt and adjust to cope with the situations they find themselves in because their men have failed them.

Also in the New Testament there are several instances where Jesus has compassion for widows. For example in Luke 7:11-15, Jesus stops a funeral procession of a young man. The Bible documents, 1) he was her only son, 2) she was a widow, 3) there was a large crowd with her, 4) when the Lord saw her he had compassion for her. In order for Jesus (an outsider) to gain some of the information Luke recorded, there had to be some investigation. I believe Jesus may have asked (not that he had to) about the woman and the dead person. Jesus' actions were directly connected to the realization that this woman had already lost her covenant husband. The young son represented the person whom more than likely took care of her in the absence of her husband. Jesus moved in the consistency of his Father's word and had mercy on the widow. Jesus knew that she was vulnerable and alone. His actions were purely compassionate and protective. He did not require or request of her faith in him. He did not expect or demand of her (in the midst of her grief and sorrow) anything for him to do this miracle. This is a clear example of how a covenant man deals with an uncovered, vulnerable woman. No demands, no challenge, no requirement, no exchange of services, just compassion. Jesus simply said, **"Don't cry!"** and turned to the wooden plank on which the dead boy was being carried and touches it. His command to the dead boy was, "Arise!" This resurrection can be compared to the need that exists today for men to arise and resume responsibility for the women who have been left unprotected in their absence. The young man was delivered back to his mother not for her to take care of him, but rather *for him to take care of her!*

Acts 6 describes how the church provided for the widows a daily distribution of goods. However, because of ethnic prejudice those who managed the dispersal tainted this process. Out of this arose a need to have the widows cared for by a specific group of covenant men. These men were to meet the requirements of *good reputation, full of the Holy Ghost, and wisdom* in order to be qualified for this responsibility. If we keep this in context with what we have previously established about God's divine order, we understand why a deacon can only be a male. The reason why 1 Timothy 3:8-13 states that the deacon be a husband of a faithful wife is because he will be dealing with women that he must cover and protect without personal desires or manipulation interfering. If the man is married to a faithful woman that respects him and satisfies him, there will be no concern for him when he must go out to care for a widow who needs a covenant man to cover her life. This is also why he must also be full of the Holy Ghost and wisdom. The deacon must have the adeptness to make good decisions and have good judgment concerning the woman he is covering.

This is of great importance. If a woman is not chaste or disciplined, he must be able to maintain his integrity while covering her. James 1:27 echoes that pure religion is to care for the orphans and widows in their distress while keeping oneself free from the pollution of the world. When you quantify the acts of religion, they should include care and concern for the orphans (fatherless) and widows (husbandless). These are the most vulnerable in society. God certainly has outlined consistently throughout his word, the need for the father figure or covenant man to be in place in order to secure the order that was established in Genesis and as outlined by Paul in 1 Cor. 11:3. The order has never changed. But altering that order opens the avenue for the woman to be beguiled (Gen. 3) and the children's teeth to be set on edge (refer to Jeremiah 31:29).

Even in 1st Timothy chapter 5, Paul gave insight to the issues and problems concerning widows in the church. Paul wanted them to be cared for, but he didn't want that care to be abused. Therefore, he made the distinction of who should be categorized as a true widow. At that time many young women had inherited wealth upon the death of their husbands and would not be eligible for the church's assistance though they needed a covering in their lives.

Paul also mentioned widows who had relatives and

children who could and should provide for them their daily needs. Then there were young pleasure seeking women with bad reputations, who were not trusting in the Lord. These Paul says are not true widows. Yet Paul was consistent with the Old Testament principle. The focus was that the church should be taking care of those who had no other means of protection and survival. But the burden of provision doesn't always fall on the church, sometimes the family is able or the inheritance is sufficient to meet the physical needs. Yet in 1st Timothy 5:14 Paul admonished the younger widows to marry and be covered and governed by their husbands to keep them from "turning aside to Satan". Who does that remind you of? (Clue: Gen. 3)

In essence the man must reconcile himself to the covenant and calling of headship and responsibility, so that the woman and children can return to their role and position in the divine order of the family. This order comes from God and creates the best environment for the togetherness, the harmony, the prosperity, and the blessing of a family. I believe the coming generation has the chance to incorporate these ideals into their life, since many of them have no teaching and no standard whatsoever.

Looking at the present perplexity of marriage, sexuality and relationships, this would be an ideal time to adopt a new paradigm. We still have a chance to restore hope in the minds of those who are fearful of marriage and healthy male/female association. This is our last chance to address one of the most controversial issues in the church and the world today. We need our fathers, husbands, uncles, brothers, and men to care for, love, protect, cover and have compassion for those who God has entrusted to them. Fatherless-ness is the main ingredient for a deficient family and vulnerable community and a weak church. Presently, we stand in desperate need of men to adopt families, churches, communities, cities and nations so that society can return to wholeness and God's divine order. Be a father and save a generation!

Motherless

On the other hand we have another problem that has been recognized more with each generation; it is the motherless child. The old Negro songwriter wrote, "Sometimes I feel like a motherless child, a long way from home."

Several things come to mind when I speak of the motherless child. There is the foster child, given up at birth by the mother. The reasons surrounding that scenario are numerous. Sometimes it's a teenage mother that can not take care of the child. At other times it is the drug-addicted mom who is incapable of raising a child. And occasionally it is the mother that doesn't want an unplanned child because she doesn't want the responsibility. These are just a few situations that occur today.

There is the motherless child that is the result of an incarcerated mother. This number is increasing daily and this is frightening. Children are being left to grandmothers, aunts, cousins, or foster care because the mothers are in jail.

Additionally, there is the motherless child that is a result of an untimely death. The effects of this can be long-term and difficult for the child to reconcile.

Some motherless children are a result of divorces where fathers obtain custody of the children. These cases are not as common but have increased dramatically over the years. In fact, according to the U.S. Census Bureau's 2000 census, the number of single-father families grew from 393,000 in 1970 to 2 million in 2000. This represents an increase of over 500%. During this same time period married couples with their own children decreased from 40 to 24% of American households. Within the single-father household numbers the census revealed that the large majority of them were divorced or never married.

Regardless of how the separation takes place, it is very unfortunate and in every case the child suffers. How strange it is that as a result of the physical expression of love between a man and a woman, an unwanted, unloved child can be the end result. That child having not asked to be born can be the subject of such intense rejection and suffering. Why have our priorities changed so? What is it that we feel is so much more important than the basic care and nurture of our offspring? Certainly capitalism and self-indulgence has damaged, almost irreparably so, the fiber of our human existence. Since our society focuses so intently on individual satisfaction the byproduct tends to be the neglect of the family unit. The desire and passion to care for our own is fading, as time is exhausting.

Still the motherless child I care to deal with in this chapter is the one that is a result of the working, career minded and liberated woman. Though in some cases it seems she doesn't have a choice, this motherless child is the one that deeply concerns me. I'll explain why.

I can still taste the tomato soup with rice and crackers on the side that so often awaited me at the end of my elementary school day. Occasionally, that's what we snacked on in the colder months when we came home from school. I didn't get a key to our apartment until maybe high school, because there was really no need for one. For many of my friends and I, who grew up in the Highbridge projects in the Bronx, there was no need for a key because we had mothers that didn't work. They were always home to greet us after the school day was over.

Now I must be honest, we didn't have a lot of luxuries. Clothes and shoes were minimal. Meals where typically single servings. The only vacations I remember were by car or train to my grandmother's home or to my older brother's place to be with his family. But there was something about my mother's presence at home that made me who I am today. Her presence in fact was **invaluable**. There was a nurturing and stability that money couldn't buy. That is the value of a mother.

How many latchkey children do we have today who are being nurtured and developed by MTV or HBO in the mother's absence? How many twelve-year old girls are letting teenage boys into the house, exploring sexuality at the hands of another kid while mom is away? How many young men are leaving the books and heading to the streets to be embraced and accepted by another wayward man in a worst situation than he? How much family education is missed? How are those conversations ever retrieved? These motherless children are designing a generation of which we have no title for. So we have labeled them X and Y (why) generations. They carry their mother's last name and they are likely to repeat the mistakes of that single parent. They are extremely independent. Their philosophy is largely founded upon what they believe is right and wrong, almost disconnected from the world around them (see Proverbs 12:15). They reject conventional wisdom and advice and make decisions based on a fantasy like existence. Proverbs 14:12 says, "There is a way that seems right to a man, but its end is the way of death."

Psychologists are reporting with more evidence and support each year how the mind is most impressionable between birth and five years old. But too often children are not in the primary care of their mothers during those years. They are often in daycare for six to ten hours a day or with a babysitter or a relative and the voices they hear during those most impressionable years are widespread and varying in standards. In general we don't really trust these systems. That's why we are placing cameras everywhere and surveillance via the Internet is commonplace. We need a security measure to make up for our mothers not being present. These children are not looked at as being motherless, but in fact they are!

These motherless children are often raised in an environment where the motive for care is financial and not maternal love and a sense of family. Certainly we want to believe that the daycare worker loves children but in essence if you didn't pay them there would be no care. The uniqueness of each child is best understood by the soul that carried it for nine months. Caretaker systems cannot possibly compare in the fulfillment of the needs of the individual child.

How many more horrific cases of abuse must we endure before the message is clear that daycare centers can be dangerous? Nannies beating and shaking children, daycare workers that leave children unattended for hours with no human interaction, substandard sanitary conditions, not knowing what is going in your child's stomach, should be motivation enough for mothers to reassess this priority. My older brother would always say "Until your child can talk, don't leave them anywhere you don't feel completely comfortable." Those nurturing and development years are priceless ones.

According to the Survey of Income and Program Participation, in the fall of 1993 there were 9.9 million children under age five who were in need of child care while their mothers were working. A little more than half (52 percent) of preschool-age children were cared for by someone *other* than relatives while their mothers were at work. In 1993, more preschoolers were cared for in organized child-care facilities than in any other arrangement. Approximately

30 percent of all **preschoolers** were cared for in organized childcare facilities. The remaining 22 percent were cared for by non-relative arrangements. From 1991 to 1993 there was a seven-percent jump in dependency on organized daycare facilities according to this same survey.

Now we are well aware of the present day dilemma of children born to unwed mothers or broken homes. The U.S. Census Bureau report dated March 2000 documented that there are more than 9.6 million single mother households in a the United States. 4.1 million of them have never been married and 3.4 million of them are divorced. In addition, 3.3 million are living below the poverty line. Therefore, the woman has an obligation to work in order to survive. But there are many who chose to work simply because career, money and worldly recognition are more important than rearing and nurturing children. For some reason this is looked upon as an undesirable occupation. Yet it is invaluable to the child. Preschoolers are in the midst of forming personalities, developing cognitively, and learning social skills while the mother is at work. This growing trend of mothers working will continue to loose its validity overall as we produce more children who have less of a significant contribution to society.

This is the key to gauging the success of this part-time nurturing generation of mothers. The question is where is the greatness? Where are the inventions that offer society good beyond financial gain? Values, substance, morality, integrity, commitment, loyalty, standards, betterment of the whole, are all terminology not used or grasped by our X and Y generations. The absence of mom for breakfast and lunch will condition sons and daughters for individualism, which inevitably dilutes the importance of the family.

If you and I can get the word out, maybe we have a chance at redirecting this generation to abstinence until marriage and children only after wedlock. Surely I am the consummate optimist and some would call me foolish, however, as I have shared this message with hundreds of youth and young adults many have thanked me as they've committed to this new standard. Equally many parents have expressed their appreciation for a message that is straight forward and eye opening. They're even honest enough to admit that if they had known these things while growing up they would have made different decisions in their relationships.

Mothers look closely and carefully into your children's eyes and you will see that everything inside them says, "I NEED YOU MORE THAN ANYONE ELSE, Please don't leave me in the hands of a stranger!"

Please don't leave them **motherless!**

Can you wait for what you want?

Delight yourself in the Lord; and He will give you the desires of your heart... Psalm 37:4

One of the things that I have noticed lately is that more and more people are becoming vocal about their commitment to sexual abstinence. And I'm not talking priest and nuns. More and more people are willing to wait for what they really want. The commitment and stability of marriage with the sexual intimacy is priceless.

Not long ago I read an article in Essence magazine by Audrey Edwards entitled "Will I ever have sex again?" highlighting from a different perspective the subject of abstinence. Casual sex, faithfulness, and wanting a relationship that is enriching and long lasting were the issues of concern. But more than that my joy comes from knowing that people are coming to grips with the fact that the sexual revolution of the past 20 or 30 years has only worsened the best of us.

I've recently heard of some celebrities "coming out of the closet" so to speak about their abstinence. This is a first for me (in this generation). Most times everyone brags about his or her multiple partners and who they did last and who they want to do next and so on. Not only that but living with someone is no big deal and having children outside of marriage has obviously become acceptable. But to hear people saying I'm saving myself for my mate or returning to the values of their parents is exciting. I feel maybe that the perception is changing toward a new appreciation for sexuality in its proper context. Waiting is nothing to be ashamed of; in fact it is something to be proud of.

Try asking some of the people who didn't wait whether or not they regret it. Ask the young women who don't really know who the father of their child is. Ask the man who lies in the hospital with an incurable disease running rampant in his body, nibbling away at his youthful life. Ask the young man who had bullet wounds inflicted upon him from the jealous boyfriend, who thought he was messing with his girl. Ask the divorced parents who one or the other thought it was only a night of passion with no consequences. Ask the countless children who grew up fatherless and live a life that is a result of abandonment. Ask around, they will all tell you a different version of the same sad story, I thought illicit sex had no repercussions.

There are countless stories all stemming from immorality, fornication, adultery, and lack of trust, lack of true foundation, ignorance and selfishness. They are of every race and culture, straight and gay, young and old, religious and otherwise. We all have a story of how we would have preferred "true love" and abstinence 'til marriage. Don't ask in a crowd. Ask them privately. That way you'll hear the real story. Ask your mother or your father. Ask them, does it pay to wait? Beg of them and honest response. Ask the hooker when she is old; see what she will say. Ask the aids patient the day before he or she dies, "was it fun? Was it worth it?" Ask them, was it the best sex you ever had? Then tell me who's doing the celebrating.

Waiting is liberating. During my single years after receiving this revelation I enjoyed a new freedom when I meet a young lady. I didn't have to be overly romantic, I didn't have to kiss her, and I didn't have to say yes when she said, "I want to see you again." As I begin to share these things I realize that my past mistakes and failures were not just for me, but for others as well as myself, and why not? The Bible does record the failures of Adam, Noah, Moses, Samson, David, Solomon and countless others, why not me? These failures in marriages and relationships, in fornication and lust have now been transformed. Once they are confessed and forgiven by God, I am released from their guilt context and I use the lessons learned to release others.

It's time to celebrate the freedom from the pressure of sex before its time. There is joy in knowing my purpose as a man, as a seed bearer, as a husband, as a son, and as a man of God. Those who don't yet embrace and understand it can misunderstand this freedom. It can be misinterpreted as an escape of some sort. Or some may be jealous of it. But more than anything else the freedom is and expression and a result of knowing God's divine design of abstinence is better than the devil's package of short-term pleasure and long-term repercussions. It is indeed liberating to no longer walk in confusion about my manhood, about God's order, about marriage, about sexuality, about relationships or how so many things in life are haywire and perverted because we've never been properly instructed through life's great manual, the Bible; written by the world's greatest author, God.

Wouldn't it be wonderful to know that your child won't "just say no" not really knowing why they are saying no, or using a condom to hopefully spare themselves pregnancy, disease or exposure. Think of the joy of that "white dress" your daughter will be wearing because it truly represents the purity of an untouched, uncompromised woman. How about the joy of a father passing the covenant responsibility of his daughter to a man that knows who she is and will cover her, protect her, be responsible for and love her unconditionally.

Imagine the joy of a young man whose relationship with God dictates his relationship with his wife, his children, his community and his world. Think of how this stance will effect generations to come. Think of the children who will be given real tangible advice and information from which to build and enjoy fabulous relationships for a lifetime. Think of how many young men and women will make a choice against the false covenants of a man with a man or a woman with a woman. Think of the release from the tragic disappointments that are so often related to the entanglements of premarital sex and extra-marital affairs.

My friend, can you wait for what you want? Take a moment to consider that God's purpose for marriage, sex and relationships is designed to save you some unnecessary disappointments in these areas. Your spirit will thrive on this choice to wait for what you really want. You will be free from guilt! You will feel connected with God's purposes for your life. You will have a greater appreciation for love. Your sense of satisfaction will be unrelated to the flesh. Waiting is liberating!

Your mind and your soul will be released from their insatiable appetite of lust. You will be balanced and reasonable. You will gauge the importance of love over lust. You will focus on the higher values that lead you to healthy human interaction. You will have the power of history to depend upon to move into your future confidently. Daily you must embrace with hopeful anticipation, the introductions to new people and new scenarios that propel and development you into a deeper maturity. You will feel different, you will think different, you will react different. Waiting is liberating!

Last but not least, your body will be released. It will thrive from new leadership. It will no longer be in control. It will no longer be the leader, but rather it will follow leadership. Your soul and your mind manipulate it, and they are under the authority of your spirit. Your body will be healthy and energetic. It will serve the rest of you and it will serve your destiny. It will find comfort in knowing that the soul knows better.

Now I must warn you that your body, because of its health and energy, wants to be in its former role of leadership. However, as long as you keep feeding your spirit with the Word of God and new revelation your body will be weak in comparison to your mind, your soul, and your spirit. Hallelujah, waiting is liberating!

Uncrossing the line

Whenever I have shared this message in a church setting or youth seminar the impact has been overwhelming. In particular with the teenagers who have crossed the line of sexual intimacy, not knowing what they were getting involved with. The altar call that follows this message is designed to get people, especially young people, to make a commitment to abstinence. I ask them to come to the altar and repeat a prayer of commitment. Then before they leave the altar I ask them to shake my hand or hug me and look me in the eye and declare to the audience, and me "I will not cross that line!" or "I will not cross that line again!"

This declaration tends to be a good spiritual, psychological and emotional start down their new road of understanding. In some cases the parents have come prepared (as it may have been previously established) with chastity rings, which are worn on the ring finger of the left hand. These rings serve the purpose of a reminder of the covenant commitment, just as a wedding band serves that purpose in marriage. In some cases if the father is absent, I will serve the role of a spiritual father and place the ring on the child's finger. This has been such a powerful experience that it inevitably produces tears and hugs, bonding and sobriety in everyone that is a part of that moment.

This experience also inspires honesty in those

gathered at the altar call. Partly because I must also encourage those persons who have crossed that line, to uncross it and many people are honest enough to admit that. So as not to condemn anyone I become overly conscious of those teenagers that are no longer virgins and are sitting in a pool of guilt. The love and forgiveness of God must be emphasized so that they will be moved enough to make a new commitment. Almost without fail when they come up the tears are already flowing down and heads are held low. With the young ladies it tends to be a little more painful since they realize their hymen can not be unbroken. Yet it is the expression of love and forgiveness from a father or covenant man that restores them as a sign of God's forgiveness. With the young men the realization is a little different. Now they understand that what they have done is more than the sexual act. They have created a false covenant with a young woman. They have hurt and manipulated a young lady, instead of protecting and respecting her. They realize that crossing these lines is irreversible and it leaves a permanent mark inn her life history.

In the story of the woman caught in sexual immorality, namely adultery, in John 8:1-11 the guidelines from which we will rebuild the hope of those who have crossed that line are found. The Bible often outlines the compassion of Jesus in the New Testament to underscore the fact that God did not send Jesus to condemn the world, but that the world though Him might be saved. So the woman caught in adultery though **guilty**, is not **condemned**. So at that altar call instead of levying upon some broken heart a spirit-shattering blow, we redeem them with love. We establish that not a person in the church or on this earth can condemn you. So therefore you can come to this altar and whisper solemnly the words, "I will not cross that line again." And time and time again with tears in their eyes both young men and women have whispered those very words to me.

My hope and prayer is that many who read this book will understand the great value in choosing to abstain from sex until marriage. The spiritual and emotional damage that so often inevitably accompanies the sex act is not realized until long after the act is over. Even beyond the potential for disease and pregnancy we have to deal with the reality of the human spirit. And in doing so, we understand better how it thrives from love and companionship.

The power of the male/female relationship goes so far beyond the act of sex that the focus should be redirected to intellectual, emotional, and spiritual compatibility. The importance of my spirit thriving and being blessed from being exposed to and interacting with another becomes the springboard for a great relationship. A relationship shouldn't have to be driven to the bedroom or even to the marriage altar to be authenticated. Rather it should embrace the joy of having and enjoying a fruitful, positive, communicative friendship that may or may not lead to romance and marriage.

Now I realize that if the next generation chooses to live like this it would be bad for the talk show circuit. Ricky, Jerry, Jenny and others would definitely have to find new and more sensible topics to explore, but would that be so bad?

Not so long ago I literally sat and applauded the TV as I watched the closing moments of NYPD Blue's season premiere episode. The young blonde male officer who was caught in the midst of controversy throughout the program is at the bar after his long arduous day. Some of the other officers were picking on him about the incident that took place earlier in the day. He turns and approaches a table where a male and a female officer are seated. After commencing to dialogue with the female officer, Franco, the male officer abruptly leaves. The dialogue is insinuating yet intriguing for both. They seem to be speaking out of a sense of confusion about each other.

Finally, the blonde male officer asks Franco if she

wants to go to his place and she says yes. The next scene finds them in heated passionate engagement. They are kissing and caressing. He is topless and pulling off her blouse. The bra comes off and it seems obvious to the viewers we are about to get into a steamy sex scene that should be in an R-rated movie. Until she says, "Stop!" She continues, "Stop!" "I can't do this! This doesn't feel right!" He backs off as she puts her bra on and sits on the edge of the bed and begins to cry. He responds to her tears by holding her, and she says, "If it's okay, I just want to be held." He helps her with her clothing and fixes the pillow and the blanket and covers her. Then he lies beside her and holds her and says, "That's all I wanted too." Just to have you here, just to be together, just to hold you. I applauded.

Is it so bad to want someone to hold and not to have? Someone to squeeze but not deflower? Someone to love and not lust over? Is it so bad? Calvin Richardson and Chico De'Barge collaborate on an old song called "True Love." The lyrics say, "It's hard to find." I declare when you find it, its worth so much more than sex. I am so grateful to God for the day he allowed me to meet my wife, Maria. It is "true love" that we embrace and enjoy. To know and be known, to feel and be felt, to think of and be thought of, to love and be loved, is the greatest thing in the world. The final line of the famous jazz ballad "Nature Boy" says, "The greatest thing, you'll ever learn, is just to love and be loved in return." It's my favorite tune.

It's really wonderful to know that I can walk in a room and sense whether or not Maria is there without seeing her. To face uncertain moments with the certainty of her love is priceless. To be accused of sexual impropriety by those who thought I had compromised my standard, seemed to only to serve as a greater platform to support what I knew I had found, "true love." True love is the kind of thing that makes me forget about inappropriate sex. It is just so satisfying to know she loves me, and I love her.

Much time had passed since I had uncrossed that line. I had resolved never to cross it again unless I found the woman of my "secret" dreams and my "private" prayers (Proverbs 18:22). During my single years it was so enjoyable not having to worry about the traps and repercussions of sex. I could hug one, have dinner with another and even love some without any backlash. Once you have hurt others and been hurt yourself there is no entertainment in perpetuating the negative.

For some, it will be hard to uncross that line, for others it will be easy because you are there physically already. But for all it must be a spiritual commitment, an intellectual determination, and a physical resolution. Stay the course. Let your spirit convict and control your mind, soul, and body. Redefine who you are and who you will be to some one else. Start the trend. Set the standard. Inaugurate a new tradition. Save yourself and your generation. Give "true love" a chance. Let your spirit thrive. Abstain until marriage and wait for what you want!

Remember, for *these reasons* shall a man leave his father and mother and cleave to his wife...

Shalom...

For information regarding conferences or seminars contact:

Rev. Nathan R. Byrd
Jesus Makes the Difference Ministries, Inc.
P.O. Box 154 New York, NY 10272
or online at jmdm.org

Or contact:

The Worship Center of St. Albans
114-37 Farmers Blvd.
St. Albans, N.Y. 11412
718-468-2234

Printed in the United States
38677LVS00002BA/67-216